Research Methodology

John Kuada

Research Methodology

A Project Guide for University Students

Samfunds
litteratur

John Kuada
Research Methodology. A Project Guide for University Students.

1st edition 2012
© Samfundslitteratur 2012

COVER Imperiet
TYPESET SL grafik, Frederiksberg (www.slgrafik.dk)
PRINT Narayana Press, Gylling (www.narayana.dk)
ISBN 978-87-593-1554-5

Samfundslitteratur
Rosenørns Allé 9
DK-1970 Frederiksberg C
Tlf.: +45 3815 3880
Fax: +45 3535 7822
slforlagene@samfundslitteratur.dk
www.samfundslitteratur.dk

All rights reserved. No part of this book may be reproduced or transmitted in any form or by any means, electronic or mechanical, including photocopying, recording, or by any information storage or retrieval system, without permission in writing from the publisher. This does not include short excerpts for review.

CONTENTS

Acknowledgements	9
Foreword	11
Introduction	13

Part 1 Basic Guidelines for Group Work and Project Writing — 17

Chapter 1 Problem- and Project-based Learning — 19
- Introduction — 19
- The Scandinavian Approach to Problem-based Learning — 20
- Problem-oriented Studies — 20
- Project-organised Teaching — 21
- Group Studies — 22
- Integration of Theory and Practice — 23
- Key Points — 23

Chapter 2 The Group Process — 25
- Introduction — 25
- Belbin's Typology of Team Roles — 25
- Initial Tasks in Group Process Development — 30
- The Role of a Supervisor — 33
- Key Points — 33

Chapter 3 The Project Work Process — 35
- Introduction — 35
- Research as an Iterative Process — 35
- Choosing the Project Theme — 37

Choosing the Topic	37
Problem Formulation	38
Literature Review and Justification of the Research	40
Research Strategy and Resources	41
Objectives of Your Study	42
Key Points	43

Chapter 4 Structure of Your Project Report — 45

Introduction	45
A General Project Structure	45
Deciding on the Contents of your Chapters and Paragraphs	53
Key Points	53

Part 2 Project Design and Theoretical Platform — 55

Chapter 5 Research Design — 57

Introduction	57
The Four Levels of Understanding	57
Exclusive versus Complementary Approaches	60
Key Points	62

Chapter 6 The Role of Theories in Your Project — 63

Introduction	63
What is a Theory?	64
Classification of Theories	64
Use of Theories	67
Guidelines for Literature Review	68
Key Points	69

Chapter 7 Metatheories, Paradigms, and Philosophy of Science — 71

Introduction	71
The Concept of Paradigm	71
Objective-Subjective Perspectives in Social Science	72
Classifications of Paradigms in Social Science	74
Key Points	89

Part 3 Methods and Techniques 91

Chapter 8 Qualitative Data Collection Methods and Techniques 93
General Characteristics of Qualitative Methods 93
Qualitative Data Collection Techniques 95
Challenges in Collecting Qualitative Data 99
Evaluation of Qualitative Studies 100
Key Points 101

Chapter 9 Quantitative Data Collection Methods and Techniques 103
Introduction 103
General Characteristics of Quantitative Methods 103
Steps in Quantitative Data Collection 105
Quantitative Data Collection Techniques 107
Evaluating Quantitative Studies 114
Key Points 115

Chapter 10 Mixed Research Methods 117
Introduction 117
Similarities and Differences between Quantitative
and Qualitative Methods 117
Mixing Quantitative and Qualitative Methods 119
Triangulation 121
Examples of Mixed Methods 122
Key Points 124

Chapter 11 Summary, Reflections, and Further Readings 125
Introduction 125
Problem Formulation or Research Questions 125
Project Structure and Style of Writing 126
Literature Review and Theories 126
Philosophy of Science and its Influence on Your Project 127
Methods 128
Self-Assessment and Reflection 128
For Further Reading 129

Bibliography 133

Subject Index 137

ACKNOWLEDGEMENTS

First of all, I am grateful for the inspiration and wisdom of many of my colleagues at Aalborg University and elsewhere whose critical questions and suggestions have shaped my thoughts on project work and research methods, as well as the contents of this book.

My colleague, Professor Olav Jull Sørensen, has provided friendly and professional advice and encouragement. Michael Simonsen has provided me with valuable secretarial assistance and Gitte Thomsen has corrected my English. Annette Kjølby of Samfundslitteratur has read through several versions of the manuscript and helped me think through my arguments. My head of department, Mrs. Birgitte Gregersen, has been kind enough to write the foreword to the book. I owe all of them a profound debt of gratitude.

I am also grateful for many students at Aalborg University who have tested this material and have given feedback and encouragement.

But the people I owe most gratitude to are my wife, Gitte Thomsen, and our children who have had to bear my occasional lack of social attention when working on the book. They provided me with understanding, support, and encouragement when I needed them most. To them I extend my sincere thanks.

John Kuada
Aalborg, January 2012

FOREWORD

Problem- and project-based learning (PBL) is a key pedagogical approach to teaching since it helps students become effective real-life problem solvers in organisations. Problem-based learning emphasises cooperative learning. Students actively participate in their learning process as they choose theories, models, and methods that they consider to be necessary to solve the "real-world" problem that they have agreed to address (under the guidance of competent and experienced supervisors).

At Aalborg University we have observed that students who have backgrounds in traditional forms of university education find this problem-based pedagogy highly challenging. It is in this context that we see the contribution of John Kuada's book: *Research Methodology – A guide to University Students*. The book provides a "hand-holding" guide to students that do not have any, or only very little, previous experience with problem-based learning.

A major strength of the book is the simplicity and straightforwardness of the language used. This approach is quite inviting and provides students a friendly introduction to relatively complex ideas and methods. The book speaks to students directly and therefore encourages their engagement in the process of learning about how they can justify the various choices they make in their project work process.

The book draws on Professor John Kuada's many years as lecturer and supervisor for students in the department of economics and business administration, and I believe that the book will serve as a useful reading for any students who are looking for a step-by-step pathway for their project work.

Birgitte Gregersen
Head of Department
Department of Business and Management
Aalborg University
Denmark

January, 2012

INTRODUCTION

Many universities today require their social science students to write projects at various stages in their educational process. Through these projects you (as students) are expected to demonstrate your understanding of contemporary concepts and theories and to apply them to solve identified social science problems, and to create new knowledge. What steps should you take to attain this objective? This is the subject matter taken up in this book. Consequently, it is a book about the use of research methods in your projects. In other words, it aims to help you develop comprehensive research strategies for your projects. In addition to presenting methods and techniques for data collection it provides an introduction to issues of philosophy of science as applied in the social sciences. I have adopted this approach because during the last twenty years my interactions with students from different parts of the world have convinced me that many students need to have a fair understanding of the root assumptions that guide researchers in their investigations and how these assumptions inform their theoretical thinking and choice of methods. That is, students need to know that social science researchers have developed different ways of understanding social issues. These different ways of understanding are premised on different assumptions that guide what these scientists consider to be "real", and thereby influence the direction of their investigations.

There are many textbooks in research methods that may provide you with some guidelines. But most of them are either very technical or very philosophical. Many students who consult these books for guidance therefore become immensely frustrated. With this in mind, and particularly drawing upon my capacity as the director of two master's degree programmes in business economics at Aalborg

University, I consider it purposeful to write this book to help you find your project work process a lot more enjoyable. While most of the illustrative examples are drawn from business economics, the target groups of the book include those of you who are doing bachelor and master's degree programmes in other social science disciplines as well.

The book is divided into three parts. The first part covers the first four chapters. Chapter one introduces you to the concept of problem- and project-based learning (PBL) as a pedagogical approach, now extensively practised in many European and some North American universities. This approach to learning helps students become effective real-life problem solvers in organisations through project work and theory-practice integration. Chapter two discusses the various roles that students play in their groups when they work together on specific projects. Reading this chapter will enable you to understand your and your peer's behaviour and help you adopt response behaviours that are positively reinforcing rather than energy sapping. The third chapter introduces you to the project work process, identifying some of the key components of the process. It emphasises the iterative nature of the process and seeks to help you minimise the frustrations that you may experience when aspects of these activities appear to you to be too slow. Chapter four provides you with specific guidelines on how to structure your project report and ensure coherence in your arguments. It is always important for you to remember that when examiners read your reports, the meaning the reports convey to them will depend on the structure and logical flow of your work. This is why efforts must be made to ensure that the various chapters and paragraphs are linked together and contain only the information and message that is relevant to the problems that you seek to address in your project.

Part two of the book discusses research design and the role of theories in research projects. It contains three chapters. Chapter five discusses research design and how this can be presented as the methodology chapter in your project. It identifies four levels of presentation, starting with ontology, moving through epistemological considerations to methodological approaches, and ending with the choice of techniques. Chapter six presents a classification of theories in the social science literature and discusses what roles theories can play in your project. Chapter seven discusses the concept of paradigm or what Abnor and Bjerke (2009) refer to as the "ultimate presumptions" of social science scholars. It provides a brief introduction to some of the contemporary classifications of paradigms in social science as well as the key definitional concepts adopted in the literature. The aim of the chapter is to introduce you to a variety of paradigms that can inspire the presentation of your views of reality and guide your research strategy formulation.

Part three contains four chapters that are devoted to specific methods and techniques of data collection and analysis. Chapter eight introduces you to the methods and techniques that are frequently used to collect qualitative data. A similar introduction to quantitative methods and techniques is provided in chapter nine. Chapter ten discusses the possibilities of mixing both methods. Chapter eleven pulls together the various discussions in the book and draws your attention to issues requiring more elaborate treatment. It also provides you with an annotated list of readings that will provide deeper insights into some of these issues. Together, the eleven chapters provide a concise knowledge base that will enable you to write an academic project with less uncertainty about what your teachers expect from you in the project work process.

PART 1
BASIC GUIDELINES FOR GROUP WORK AND PROJECT WRITING

Group-based project work is based on the view that students learn best when they work together to solve problems rather than follow direct instructions from their teachers. In this way students make sense of new concepts by themselves more quickly and relate the theories that they learn more readily to practical problems. Part one of the book therefore gives you insight into the rationale underlying this approach to learning, and provides you with some guidelines on how to manage the learning process and write a good project together with your fellow students. It consists of four chapters. Chapter one introduces you to the concept of problem- and project-based learning (PBL), emphasising the benefits of group work. Chapter two informs you about the group process and draws your attention to some of the challenges in working in groups. Chapter three introduces you to the project work process as well as the major characteristics of a good project. Chapter four provides you with some guidelines about how to structure your project.

CHAPTER 1
PROBLEM- AND PROJECT-BASED LEARNING

INTRODUCTION

Traditional universities have repeatedly been criticised for placing their staff and students in an ivory tower. In other words, they detach their students from the messiness of real-world problems. Problem- and project-based learning (PBL), as a pedagogical approach, attempts to address this criticism. It trains students to become engaged problem solvers. It does so by providing authentic experiences that foster active learning, and support knowledge creation and a natural integration of university-level learning and real-life experience. In other words, it encourages students to identify the root problems in specific social or organisational settings, understand conditions needed for solving them, and design appropriate solutions. In this way, students are able to strengthen their ability to become self-directed learners. Teachers serve as facilitators of the learning process, acting more as problem-solving colleagues who nurture an environment that supports the open inquiry of their students rather than being teachers in the traditional sense. Projects are, therefore, essential parts of this approach to learning.

The intellectual background of PBL dates back to such ancient scholars as Plato and Socrates. They are reported to have insisted that their students retrieve information for themselves, search for new ideas, and debate them in a scholarly environment. Similarly, modern versions of PBL encourage students to initiate their learning processes with problems that organisations, employees, and ordinary people grapple with in real-life settings. For example, students in business management may be given organisational problems to solve. To do so, they must diagnose the situation in the same manner as an expert consultant, interviewing key players, reviewing available documents, and seeking guidance and inspiration from relevant theories, while paying attention to the assumptions underlying these theories.

This chapter introduces you to the key elements in the Scandinavian approach to PBL as a pedagogical approach. It also draws your attention to the strengths and challenges of this form of learning. In this way it prepares you for studying in Scandinavian universities in particular, but also in universities in other countries where the PBL approach is practised.

THE SCANDINAVIAN APPROACH TO PROBLEM-BASED LEARNING

Many institutions of higher education in Denmark, Norway, and Sweden have embraced PBL as a useful approach to learning. The Scandinavian version of PBL is guided by the following four *principles:*

- ▶ Problem-oriented studies
- ▶ Project-organised teaching
- ▶ Group studies
- ▶ Integration of theory and practice

PROBLEM-ORIENTED STUDIES

Professors that supervise student projects always encourage their students to be very specific about the problems they intend to solve in their project works. The guiding understanding is that students' choice of theories and methods in their projects should be based on the nature of the specific problems to be addressed. But what is a problem? Let us take the example of a business degree student. He contacts the manager of a small company for a possible project topic.

The manager informs him that his company has been experiencing declining sales over the previous two years and would like the student to help the company develop a strategy to address the problem. The student therefore initiates his project by formulating his tentative two-part problem statement as follows:

1. Why is company X experiencing declining sales in market Y?
2. Which strategies should management adopt to reverse the trend?

But is this a good problem formulation? Abnor and Bjerke (2009) remind us that what is seen as a problem depends on perception and reflection on the situation, and the ultimate assumptions underlying this reflection. This is an important point. It means that the student in the example above must be aware of the unspoken assumptions that underlie the manager's views on declining sales when discussing his or her research issues. For example, the manager may assume that his or her company's sales decline is exclusively due to changes in competition, demand, and government regulations (i.e., changes within the operational environment). To him or her, an understanding of these changes should help the company solve the problem. In other words, the manager assumes that the problem is outside the company. If the student is aware of the manager's assumptions he or she will discuss the validity of the assumption with the manager. This discussion may also help the manager to reflect on his or her own assumptions. It will also help the student and the manager to arrive at a more precise formulation of the problem that the manager would like the student to work on. The student will therefore be able to carry out an investigation that is consistent with the perceived reality of the manager.

PROJECT-ORGANISED TEACHING

As noted above, the PBL approach encourages you to learn through project assignments. A key consideration here is that you must consider the project to be relevant to the programme you are studying, and it must enhance your professional profile on graduation. Working on projects helps you connect your theoretical knowledge to practical (real-life) problems and thereby gain skills in the application of theories as problem-solving instruments.

In Scandinavian universities, student project work may be very elaborate—covering fifty to seventy pages—or may be limited to twenty pages. Students may also be required to engage in specific experiments as a basis for writing their reports.

A project, in this regard, usually starts with a problem formulation as described above. It could relate to solving a problem (or set of problems) for a company, an organization, or institution. It can also be a general social problem that attracts the curiosity and intellectual interest of the students.

GROUP STUDIES

If you are studying at a Scandinavian college or university, you are most likely to write your project in groups. The group work process has been adopted as a pedagogical approach for several reasons. First, it approximates real-life work situations in companies and organizations in the sense that employees are usually encouraged to work in teams; thus, the group work at the university exposes you to the challenges of group dynamics and multicultural group work processes. Second, you gain training in brainstorming and presenting your viewpoints to fellow students. Third, you experience the varieties of implicit assumptions that your fellow students hold and how these assumptions influence their interpretations of problems. This is usually revealed through individual students' arguments and justifications of their viewpoints. The group discussions offer you some insight and training in how to listen and interpret viewpoints of work colleagues, enabling you to not only understand other people's viewpoints but to draw their attention to the hidden assumptions underlying their viewpoints. Finally, group work experience is interesting and motivating because you become actively involved in the work and are held accountable for your actions by other group members.

The convention in most Scandinavian universities is to encourage students to form project groups of three to five students. Each group has an academic supervisor whose role is to guide the group through the process of conceiving, investigating, and writing the project. In other words, the supervisor functions as a sparring partner rather than as a director. He or she neither controls nor withdraws from the student's problem-solving process.

INTEGRATION OF THEORY AND PRACTICE

Scholars normally present their understanding of aspects of social phenomena in general statements, using terminology, concepts, and theories. These general statements may not fully reflect specific realities that you may want to investigate. You will therefore be required to reflect on how adequately the theories that you are taught during your courses explain the reality under investigation; and if they do not, you are expected to suggest modifications to the existing theories and apply them to your research questions. This process is termed *theory-practice integration*. This process encourages a coproduction of knowledge in which theories help to explain current practices, and in turn help to guide practices in a meaningful and purposeful manner. Investigations of this nature speak to both academics and practitioners, and are usually referred to as *actionable knowledge*.

KEY POINTS

In sum, PBL is based on the belief that robust knowledge and understanding occurs through dialogue, activity, and interaction around meaningful problems and tools. It has the following advantages compared to conventional approaches to education:

- ▶ It helps you to become a more motivated and independent learner with a deeper subject understanding.
- ▶ It encourages collaborative learning.
- ▶ It develops both your problem-solving skills and skills in critical analysis, communication, and group work.

There are a number of preconditions associated with effective implementation of a PBL approach to education in Scandinavian colleges and universities.

- ▶ You must be prepared to assume responsibility for your own learning.
- ▶ You must be prepared to handle the frustrations of not finding the exact solutions for your problems in existing textbooks.
- ▶ You must accept the fact that your supervisors are facilitators of your learning process. As such, they may not have ready answers to all your problems.

CHAPTER 2
THE GROUP PROCESS

INTRODUCTION

As noted in chapter one, an essential component of the Scandinavian pedagogy is group or team learning. Working in a group with individuals with unique personalities and skills can pose tremendous challenges for those of you who have limited experience in Scandinavian educational culture. This chapter draws on research in personality types and group processes to describe the typical cognitive resources that individuals bring into group work. It should help you understand the behaviour of yourself and others in the group, and in turn help you maximise the resources in the group and minimise conflicts that may arise from negative individual behaviour.

BELBIN'S TYPOLOGY OF TEAM ROLES

Belbin (1981, 1993) has shown that the success and failure of groups in achieving their goals as a team depends less on the intellectual capabilities of the group members than on their roles and behaviours. The best performing team is the one in which the members adopt positive attitudes about their roles and contribute their utmost to attaining the goals of the group. These roles are classified as *action-oriented, intellectual,* and those that involve *people skills.* Each person plays a mix of roles at various stages in the work process. The discussions here are based on Belbin's thoughts, but drawing on my observations of group work processes at Aalborg University, I have sub-divided the categories from three generic roles into six:

- A leader
- An innovator
- A thought developer
- A team organizer
- A completer
- A free rider

Table 2.1 provides a summary of the relative strengths and weaknesses associated with each of these roles.

ROLE TYPE	STRENGTHS	CHALLENGES
The Leader	Mature, confident, and pragmatic; clarifies goals; promotes decision making; delegates, but assumes control if necessary	Has a strong ego and tendency to be manipulative; thrives on verbal admiration and gratitude from teammates
The Innovator	Creative, imaginative, unorthodox, and able to solve difficult problems	Can be somewhat inflexible; sticks to own convictions
The Thought Developer	Sober, strategic, and discerning; sees all options and judges with analytical brilliance	Lacks drive and ability to inspire others; can be too critical and difficult to persuade
The Team Organiser	Cooperative, mild, and diplomatic; listens, builds, and averts friction	Can be indecisive in crunch situations
The Completer	Painstaking, conscientious, and anxious; searches out errors and omissions and delivers on time	Inclined to worry unduly and is reluctant to delegate
The Free-rider	Contributes narrowly, where he or she has special talents; dwells on technicalities	Aloof and disinterested; off-loads personal work on others; uses personal situations as excuse; plays on group sympathy

Table 2.1. Strengths and Weaknesses of Individual Roles in Group Work Processes

It must be pointed out that one member of the group can have more than one of the above attributes. He or she may, therefore, play different roles at various stages in the work process. Even in a group of three, all six attributes can be present. What is necessary is that the group members are aware of the behaviour that their colleagues express and are able to interpret the positive contributions that such behaviour can make to the total group effort.

It is also highly advisable for group members to keep in touch with each other frequently, and note the progress that individuals are making with their assignments. If someone is having trouble completing his or her part, the group must assist him or her to figure out how to solve the problem. The group as a whole must be supportive and helpful. At the same time, it must be clear to each group member that the entire group is depending on everyone doing his or her part.

The attributes outlined in table 2.1 are discussed in detail below.

The Leader

A *leader* type of person displays powers of control and coordination of the resources within the group. He or she tends to operate on a democratic, participatory basis, but is ready and able to assume rather more direct control when it feels necessary. He or she is adept at recognising and using resources within the group, and balancing its strengths and weaknesses. The leader usually has a good deal of trust and belief in people and sees their talents as useful resources, and not as threats to the role that he or she has carved out. The person in this role tends to be more concerned with practicalities and feasibility than with imaginative leaps of thought. He or she may not be the formally nominated leader of the group. Persons with such character traits must, despite their ego, know which part to play and when to play it in order to avoid undue conflict with the group.

The Innovator

The *innovator* is the "ideas person". He or she thinks constructively.

That is, their strength lies in the capacity to advance new ideas and strategies; this person brings new insights to bear on the problems and issues discussed. Such a creative mind is doubtlessly essential in solving complex social problems. This type of person has, however, other personality traits that make him or her difficult to work with. They are highly resistant to persuasion, show an unflinching belief in the rightfulness of their ideas and feel hurt about what they consider as unfavourable criticism of their ideas. Innovators are also usually undiplomatic in their reactions towards other group members owing to their assertive self-confidence and uninhibited self-expression. Many group members may therefore find themselves engaged in heated arguments with such a person, a process that can, at times, be very frustrating. There is the danger that such a person will opt out of the group if his or her ideas are persistently rejected. It is therefore necessary for other group members to exercise tolerance and try to examine the positive elements in the ideas he or she puts forward rather than uncritically rejecting them because they may sound outrageous. Sometimes the misunderstandings between the innovator and the group are due to lack of clarity of expression. It is the task of the group leader to listen critically to the discussions, pick up the essential points, and present them in a manner that enables other group members to gain the insight that the new ideas provide.

The Thought Developer
Relationships between the innovator and other group members will be substantially improved if the group has a person with the attribute of the *thought developer*. The strength of the thought developer lies in his or her ability to think critically, to analyse ideas and suggestions, and to evaluate their feasibility in terms of solving the problem at hand. This person is usually a very serious, critical, and objective person who is very sober in his or her reflections. He or she may not have a highly creative mind of his or her own but be incredibly keen in discerning the merits of ideas presented and moulding

them to suit the requirements of the group. But these traits have their negative sides as well. The person may tend to be overly critical, and like the innovator, difficult to persuade once he or she takes a standpoint. If he or she is not careful they can lower the morale in the group and use their faculties in a counterproductive manner. On the other hand, without their critical mind, asking thought-provoking questions, the group may become complacent with any first idea that an innovator introduces that has been accepted by the majority. It is therefore important to listen to the thought developer rather than brushing off his or her criticisms without careful analysis. It can save the group from ending up in blind alleys later in the work process.

The Team Organiser

The *team organiser* is the social mixer type of person. He or she is perceptive of the feelings, needs, and concerns of other group members, observing and promoting their strengths and minimising their weaknesses. His or her presence therefore raises the spirit of the group, diffuses tense situations, and provides a positive outlook on the work. With timely comments and jokes, this person helps to blunt the sharp edges of arguments between other group members. By reducing the friction, he or she makes communication within the group easier and makes the team members feel like meeting again after long hours of heated arguments. Team organisers may not contribute brilliant ideas or provide incisive critiques, but their presence is a great asset to their groups.

The Completer

The *completer* helps the group follow an agreed upon timetable and compels individual members to take deadlines seriously; to contribute inputs expected of them or face the sanctions that might be agreed upon by the group. In other words, the group rarely gets careless or overconfident if there is a completer in their midst. He or she keeps the group on its toes, so to speak. This person is highly anxious, often compulsive, introverted, and tense, and is eager to get the project completed, always reminding other group members of the submission date. But he or she does not compromise on standards. The completer can be very much irritated by the arguments generated by others and may also accuse the team leader of not taking the role seriously. All of this is aimed at communicating a sense of urgency and purpose in all group deliberations.

The completer is not the easiest person to deal with. He or she can irritate other group members with persistent nagging, and some group members would want to socially isolate him or her. The team leader must notice such developments and take up a discussion with the individual members in private, or pose the problem for group discussion.

The Free-rider

The group work process assumes that all individual members of the group contribute to the best of their ability to the collective action of the group (i.e., by producing a well-written project). But some individuals may want a free ride on the efforts of other group members by contributing nothing or making an insignificant contribution. The *free-rider's* actions may demotivate other individuals, restraining them from contributing their utmost, because they feel that the free-rider is likely to gain the same benefits as those who make the effort to write the project. It will be in the group's interest to draw the supervisor's attention to the situation at the beginning of the project. The supervisor will then assist the group to deal with the situation according to the rules of the university.

INITIAL TASKS IN GROUP PROCESS DEVELOPMENT

Well-functioning groups make deliberate efforts to grant voice to each individual in the group and make everyone feel connected. They also require specific rules of behaviour that are agreed upon by the group during the initial stages of its formation and modified when necessary. The rules ensure discipline in the group and facilitate task accomplishment.

Groups normally go through several stages in their development process and are described in the management literature using the following terms (see Komives *et al.* 1998):

▶ Forming
▶ Initial Norming
▶ Storming
▶ Further Norming
▶ Performing

Forming

When students agree to work together they must use their first meeting to develop their relationships with one another. Asking about each other's backgrounds and expectations for the group work is always a useful starting point. They must not take it for granted that each of them has the same kind of academic ambitions regarding the project work.

They must also arrange a social activity during the initial stages of the group work, even if they are under severe pressure to get their project work started. A social activity allows group members to get to know each other in a more relaxed atmosphere and to begin to gain some awareness about individual comfort zones.

Initial Norming

It is also important for the group to decide on specific rules and working procedures. Issues such as how frequently the group should meet, where meetings should be held, and for how long must be discussed and agreed upon. It is also important to decide on communication procedures. These may include rules relating to how information among group members should be disseminated, how delayed arrivals of individuals at arranged meetings should be communicated, et cetera. Some groups may consider it important to stipulate penalties for infringing upon specific rules of the group. Discussing these issues up front will help group members reduce conflicts and irritations due to the behaviour of individual group members during later stages of the work process.

Storming

Even if the rules have been agreed upon during the formation stage, the group will inevitably enter a storming stage at some point in the group work process. During this stage of group development, interpersonal conflicts arise and differences of opinion about the group and its goals will surface. If the group is unable to clearly state its purposes and goals, or if it cannot agree on shared goals, the group may collapse at this point. For example, this means that the research issue that the group should work on (i.e., the group's problem statement) must be agreed upon as quickly as possible. This will give the group a clearer focus in its work process.

Further Norming

When conflicts arise the group reassesses the effectiveness of its existing rules in ensuring smooth work processes. Some rules will be maintained while others will be modified to fit the realities of the group's process and ambitions. Free-riders may be required to vacate the group while the remaining group members reorganise themselves and reconfirm their accepted rules of behaviour and sanctions for deviations. It is also important for the group to clarify expectations of individuals and of the group as a whole, and reconfirm their work procedures and timetable.

Performing

During this final stage of development, issues related to roles, expectations, and norms are no longer of major importance. The group is now focused on its task, working intentionally and effectively to accomplish its goals.

THE ROLE OF A SUPERVISOR

It was hinted above that working on a project is an independent student exercise under the supervision of an academic staff member. The role of the supervisor is one of a facilitator rather than a director. He or she guides the learning process by asking critical questions and making suggestions that help the group to re-examine their thoughts on the problem of investigation. It is not his or her responsibility to define the problem of investigation, find the relevant literature, or edit the work. If he or she does any of these things, the group must see it as a kind gesture rather than an obligation. The supervisor's contribution to the group's learning process will be greatly facilitated if the group presents its views clearly and specifies the problems and/or doubts that confront its members. By involving the supervisor in the discussion the group members may be able to improve their perceptions of the issues and move forward with their work.

Most supervisors would like you to present them with a summary of your discussions and the issues on which you require their opinion. This may cover a few pages. You must avoid sending twenty to thirty pages to your supervisor each time you request a meeting without clearly specifying which issues/problems you would like the supervisor to discuss with you.

It is important for you to exhibit self-discipline in your relationship with your supervisor. For example, you must arrive at the agreed time when you arrange a meeting. It is also important for you to contact your supervisor when you are stuck in your work process. If supervisors are not made aware of difficulties, they cannot provide the support that you may otherwise get.

KEY POINTS

Although there are many advantages in learning together in a group, student groups nearly always face serious challenges for a variety of reasons. Irrespective of the reasons for conflicts, you must face the challenges and tackle problems in order to produce a good project and enrich your interpersonal relational experiences. This chapter offers you the following guidelines:

- Be conscious of the varieties of roles that you and your group mates play at various stages of the project.
- Emphasise the strengths of each individual in order to build positive synergy within the group.
- Engage in deliberate and open discussions of conflicts within the group to help the group move forward with the task.
- Group members must design deliberate strategies to manage the group development process (i.e., manage the forming, norming, storming and performing process).
- Remember that your supervisor is a facilitator and not a team leader.

CHAPTER 3
THE PROJECT WORK PROCESS

INTRODUCTION

A very important first step in the project work process is choosing the right topic and research issues that you want to investigate. This chapter seeks to help you make these important decisions regarding your choice of research themes and topics and to guide you through your problem formulation process. It also guides you about what to do when you get stuck in the process due to unforeseen circumstances. When you decide to work on a topic or a problem that captures the interest of all students in the group, this will motivate you to be fully engaged in the work. It will also stimulate positive interaction and discussions within your group.

The chapter also discusses the iterative nature of a project work process. That is, as you read further about the project and continue work on the problem you have initially formulated, you will discover newer dimensions and perspectives to the problem. This will make it necessary for you to modify the problem.

RESEARCH AS AN ITERATIVE PROCESS

A research process is not a straight line. It is iterative. Your group must therefore develop its own logic of investigation. This will help you to determine issues that are essential and guide you to the sources of information required for your analysis. As your project progresses, you and your group members will acquire new knowledge and improve your perception of the issues that you investigate. You will then be able to take a fresh look at some of the ideas and viewpoints that you have earlier expressed and to modify them in the light of your improved knowledge. Even your research questions (i.e., problem formulation) are likely to change as new information is acquired about the issues that you are investigating. This is an essential dimension of the learning process based on project work.

Start writing drafts of the various chapters of your project as soon as to you have agreed on the research issues to investigate. This will give you the opportunity to think through your arguments several times during the project work process. If you begin the writing process only after all data have been collected you will realize that you will run out of time and you cannot read through the project carefully before submitting it. This can have disastrous consequences for the quality of the project.

In figure 3.1 I have summarized the iterative project work process:

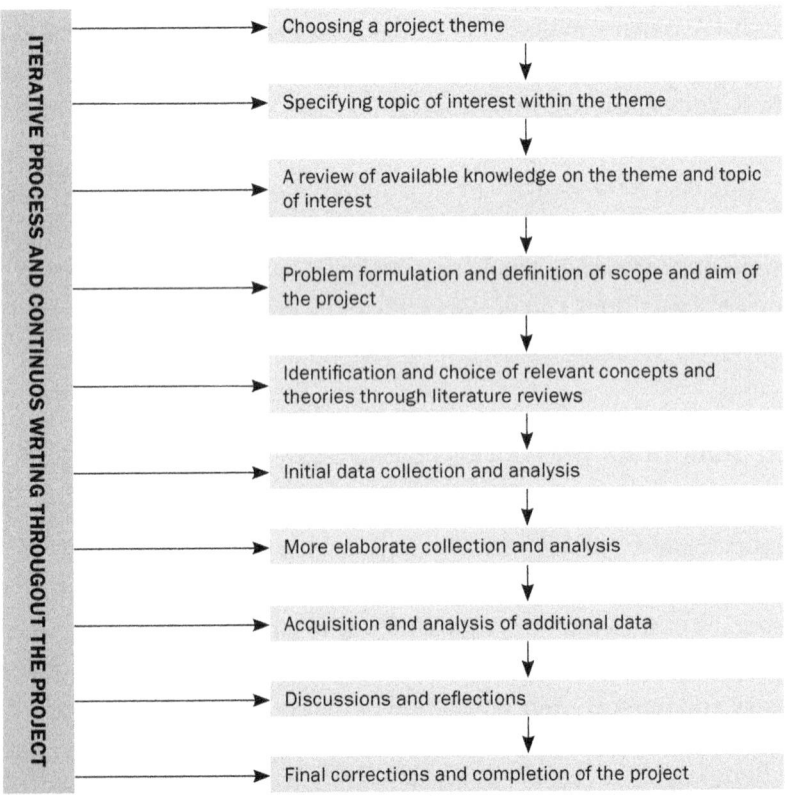

Fig. 3.1. A Schematic Illustration of a Project Work Process

CHOOSING THE PROJECT THEME

The first decision that your group has to make is which theme in your field of study you consider interesting for your project. For example, if you are students of international business you may consider these themes as relevant areas for your study:

1 International industry analysis
2 Analysis of the international competitive advantages of small firms
3 Export marketing and market analysis
4 Foreign direct investment
5 Development of international organisations
6 International human resource management
7 Intercultural management

Each of the themes listed above draws attention to a set of specific issues that have relevance for understanding the strategies, operations, and performance of international businesses, but they are too general for a good research project.

CHOOSING THE TOPIC

Having decided on the theme of investigation you can proceed to choose a topic that captures your interest. For example, if you choose industry analysis as a theme, you will have to decide which particular industry or industries will be the focus of your investigation. Similarly, several topics may be considered under export marketing, such as the mode of entry into foreign markets, or the motives and process of internationalisation.

The topic must be considered relevant and intellectually stimulating for all group members. That is, there should be a strong desire in each member to work on that topic. You must therefore engage in elaborate discussions of the various topics of interest of the individual group members. These discussions will initially cover a wide range of interests, but you will eventually realise the similarities in your interests and be able to agree on a topic that all of you consider relevant to investigate.

Fisher (2010) provides a six-stage process model to guide students in choosing a project topic. These are reproduced in box 3.1 for a quick reference.

> **Box 3.1. Process for Choosing Research Topic**
> 1. Identify a broad topic of interest
> 2. Determine the scope
> 3. Discuss the key issues, puzzles, and questions that arise from the topic
> 4. Map and structure these issues to see their interconnections
> 5. Reflect on the relevance/research potential of each of the issues
> 6. Frame the research questions you would like to address
>
> Source: Adapted from Fisher (2010: 35).

After deciding on the topic, you must also discuss the scope of your research: what to include and what to leave out of the project. Like other parts of the process, this is also tentative; however, doing so entails brainstorming, using lecture notes and other readings, and combining them with your personal observations and reflections. Each of the group members must participate actively in the discussions if individual interests are not to be overlooked by the others. Each suggested focus or problem must be written on a black/whiteboard and thoroughly discussed.

PROBLEM FORMULATION

Having agreed on the topic, the next stage in the project work process is to define the research questions (i.e., possible problems that will be worth investigating and/or solving within the chosen topic). I have argued earlier that research problems should, ideally, be defined in specific terms in order to avoid creating doubts in the minds of the group members as to the focus and scope of the project. But such a clear-cut definition may be nearly impossible in social science research. The problem definition must, therefore, be considered as an iterative process where new knowledge about the problem improves your perception and the clarity with which the problem can be defined.

Initially, your group must arrive at a working definition of its problem—in other words, a tentative description that highlights the central issues of investigation. For example, a group interested in analysing the pharmaceutical industry may want to examine the degree of concentration within that industry and the factors that influence relationships of companies within the industry. Another group interested in export marketing may want to investigate the market selection process of small companies in Denmark or of companies within a specific industry.

The following questions may provide you with some inspiration in formulating your problem :

- What is the background of the problem (i.e., how did it come about)?
- What has been the focus of earlier studies done in this area?
- What have these earlier studies ignored or paid limited attention to?
- What knowledge gap can be identified?
- What are the main research issues we want to focus our attention on?
- What makes these issues interesting and relevant?
- What do we hope to accomplish in the project?
- What are our strengths (and limitations/constraints) in conducting this investigation?
- Can these issues be investigated within the specified time limits?
- Can we gain access to relevant data?

Discussions along these lines will help you to provide a strong rationale for your project by demonstrating its relevance to some specific stakeholders in an organization or society or justifying the enhancement of knowledge that the study seeks to provide. This will also help you to avoid choosing a problem area that may be interesting but too broad to be handled in a satisfactory manner within a short span of time. Bear in mind that by focusing attention on selected issues you automatically ignore others. This is normal. It is, however, a good idea for you to inform your readers that you are aware of this general limitation in social science research.

Many non-Scandinavian students usually consider the problem formulation process very tiresome, boring, and a sheer waste of time. They wonder why their Scandinavian group mates cannot simply agree on an issue and just find a solution. The frustrations they experience are partly due to differences in learning traditions. It is important for the group members (both Scandinavian and non-Scandinavian) to remind themselves that the problem formulation process involves an upfront time investment, but time savings during subsequent phases of the project.

LITERATURE REVIEW AND JUSTIFICATION OF THE RESEARCH

Research must be positioned in relation to the existing body of literature and build on previous research done on the subject. This helps the researcher identify issues that have not been covered by previous researchers and therefore provides a justification for the research. A strong justification for the research motivates readers to read beyond the opening paragraph of the project. As students, you will be required to do the same. You must therefore read a bit about the topic. Scan through the contemporary literature, noting the mainstream thoughts and issues discussed, as well as the different viewpoints expressed by other scholars on the issue. In this way you will be able to contribute in a lively and constructive manner to the discussions at your group meetings and help your group to bring several different perspectives to bear on the issues discussed. It will also be useful to involve the group's supervisor in the discussions and to draw on other academic staff members that may have some knowledge of the issues that you consider worth investigating. The involvement of these people in the discussion at this stage of the research process will help your group settle misunderstandings that might arise.

Having agreed on the issues to investigate, your group can now plan the subsequent stages of the research, including the theoretical foundations on which to base your investigations, methods to adopt to fulfil the objectives, and how to structure the entire project. I will discuss these in detail in part two of the book.

RESEARCH STRATEGY AND RESOURCES

Considering the fact that students normally have limited time and resources for their projects, you may need to discuss these resource limitations while choosing a problem for investigation. For example, there are some issues in business economics that are highly interesting, important, and may be relevant for investigation within the current business situations, but that are too resource demanding for you to undertake. From a learning perspective, it will be pedagogically more rewarding for you to work on a problem that is less ambitious in scope and novelty than to set out on an ambitious investigation that you may abandon halfway. You must therefore consider your resource limitations when defining the problem in order to avoid unpleasant surprises.

The above statements suggest that you must undertake preliminary discussion of appropriate methods of investigation at the same time as discussing the focus of the project. It is important for you to get some idea about which kinds of data are required for a satisfactory work on the various problems of interest, the sources of such data, methods of data collection, and anticipated problems in collecting them. These considerations should influence your problem formulation.

In some cases the data collection process may prove more difficult than you anticipate, even after previous elaborate discussion. You must not discontinue the project for this reason. Discuss the difficulties with your supervisor and work out an acceptable approach that will enable you to finish the project.

OBJECTIVES OF YOUR STUDY

It is important for you to state the aim of your project very clearly. This specifies what your readers should expect from reading the project. You can choose between *descriptive* and *normative* types of research. As the name implies, the aim of descriptive research is to provide a description of a particular problem under investigation. That is, the project provides a clear picture of the issues investigated. For example, your project may be about Danish companies' attitude to investment in developing countries. Such a project may provide information on the number of Danish companies investing in developing countries, the distribution of their investment in terms of size, geographical location, sector, and product. You may also describe the investment decision-making process, as well as the underlying reasons for making such investments. Further investigations may also examine whether there is any relationship between the company's size, industry of operation, investment decision, et cetera. Such an investigation can form the basis for forecasting Danish foreign investment in developing countries in subsequent years. This kind of project has a descriptive objective (or ambition), because it describes what is happening, how it is happening, and what is expected to happen in the future, based on what we know today.

On the other hand, a *normative* research project provides guidelines for decision making. That is, the project outlines what a rational decision maker should do under the identified conditions in order to attain a given objective. For instance, if the project that examines investment in developing countries had a normative aim, the group would identify mistakes made by Danish companies in their investment decision-making process and discuss the reasons for committing such errors. The project would also present suggestions for solving the problems in order to help the Danish companies make optimal use of their investment resources. A normative objective would, for instance, be appropriate when dealing with the investments of a specific Danish company in a given country or region.

A normative study will have a descriptive part, which forms the foundation for the strategy or actions proposed by the group. This means that the group will use its analysis of the situation to justify the guidelines it recommends. Many supervisors of business-related student projects encourage their students to have both descriptive and normative ambitions for the projects.

KEY POINTS

This chapter highlights the iterative nature of the project work process that you will be involved in. It also identifies some of the stages of the process and the decisions that you must make at each stage. These include: the identification of a theme and a topic, the formulation of the problems to be investigated, and the need to take your resource limitations into account in the various decisions you make.

The chapter stresses the importance of the problem formulation process and provides you with some guidelines on how to go about formulating your problem statement. The following points require particular attention:

- ▶ You (and your group) must spend adequate time discussing the research issues that you would like to investigate and formulate them in clear terms.
- ▶ You must read what other researchers have written about the issues that you would like to investigate and draw attention to the

issues that have not been covered in the previous research. This provides justification for your investigation.
- ▶ You are allowed to modify the research issues as you read more about the project and gain more insight into it.
- ▶ The entire research process is iterative. In other words, each step in the process can be revisited when new ideas or new information emerge that require a re-examination of decisions made earlier.
- ▶ The writing process must not wait until all data are collected. Drafts and notes must be written, kept, and revised continuously in order to produce a good quality project at the end of the process.
- ▶ Do not stop your project if you run into unanticipated difficulties in implementing your research plans. Discuss the problems with your supervisor. He or she will help you find appropriate solutions.

CHAPTER 4
STRUCTURE OF YOUR PROJECT REPORT

INTRODUCTION

Two of the main criteria for evaluating your final report are the relevance of the materials that you have presented in each chapter and the logical flow of your arguments. Experience shows that some students place greater emphasis on the size of the report (i.e., the number of pages) than on the relevance of the contents to the problem that they set out to investigate. Very often, the descriptive chapters that are aimed at providing background information swell up during the writing process and assume prominence over the analytical chapters. As a result, although the final report covers several pages, the substantive discussions become thin and superficial. It is therefore important for you to pay attention to each section and chapter of the project and make sure that the purpose is clearly communicated to the reader.

This chapter provides you with some guidelines in the design of the entire project. It draws your attention to the role that each chapter can play in the project. Some universities and departments provide their students with clear guidelines on how to structure student projects. In the absence of such guidelines, the structure presented in this chapter should offer you a useful guide.

A GENERAL PROJECT STRUCTURE

Box 4.1 provides you with a list of items included in a project report. This constitutes a generic structure.of a project report. Different universities and departments may deviate from this general structure by specifying a sequence of items that serves the purpose of the programme that they offer. Universities also differ in terms of text layout, section headings and sub-sections that they recommend their students to use. Follow the guidelines offered at your university.

> **Box 4.1. General Structure of the Project Report**
>
> 1. Title page
> 2. Table of contents
> 3. Abstract or executive summary
> 4. Acknowledgements
> 5. List of acronyms (if any)
> 6. Introduction
> 7. Main body of the project
>   This will usually contain several chapters including methodological, theoretical, and empirical chapters, as well as discussion and reflection chapters
> 8. Summary and conclusions
> 9. References
> 10. Appendices

Title page

The title page provides the following information

- The title of the project
- The name of the students
- The name of the study programme and the semester
- The name of the department and university

Table of Contents

The table of contents provides a list of the chapters and main sections in the project, as well as the pages on which they appear. Some universities specify different levels of headers that students must use in their projects. In the absence of specific guidelines, students may use three levels of headers. The first is the title of the chapter. The second is the title of each section (also called an *A-head*), and the third is the title of each subsection (also called a *B-head*). The contents normally contain only first-level headings, and in some cases second-level headings.

Abstract/Executive Summary

Abstracts and executive summaries are written after the report has been completed. An abstract covers just half a page. It provides a summary of the whole project, highlighting the reasons for the project, the research design, the main findings, and the conclusion. An executive summary serves the same objective but is a bit longer (two pages maximum) and is usually written by business students who would like to provide executives with a summary of their investigations. These executive summaries place emphasis on the main findings, conclusions, and recommendations.

The choice between abstract and executive summary is usually determined by the preferences of the programme director and/or supervisor of the project. You are therefore advised to read the guidelines for your programme to determine whether abstracts or executive summaries are required.

Acknowledgements

The acknowledgement section offers you an opportunity to express your gratitude to those who have supported you in the research process, which may include organisations, companies, managers, and other officers that have granted you interviews or supported you by providing other forms of data. You may also offer thanks to persons and organisations that have granted you financial assistance in connection with the project.

List of Tables

As an aid to the reader, it may be a good idea to provide a list of all tables included in the project for a quick overview, but this is not obligatory.

List of Acronyms

Acronyms are popularly known names of institutions made up from the first letters of their official names or titles. Examples include the UN, NATO, WTO, EU, and OECD. You may also create your own acronyms as short versions of names of organisations that appear in the project. It is purposeful to provide a list of these acronyms and what they officially cover so that the reader can quickly reference them when he or she is in doubt.

Introduction

The introductory chapter should contain the following information:

- Background and justification of research issues.
- Brief outline of the structure of the project and links between the chapters.

You must specify the domain of your research in the opening paragraph of the introduction. This paragraph should highlight the importance of the research topic and why it deserves academic attention. The immediate justification of the research topic will motivate readers to read beyond the opening paragraph.

The second paragraph should help you to further develop the research problem. As noted in chapter three, researchers normally do so by locating the issues of investigation in the existing literature on the topic, by providing a brief but focused review of the available literature. This paragraph indicates the current state of knowledge in the area and what is important to know but not yet known. Remember that a study cannot be justified on the grounds that it has not been done previously.

You will normally start writing the introductory chapter of the project right from the beginning of the project work. But remember that you cannot fully introduce the project until you have finished your work. The initial drafts of the introductory chapter will provide you with a direction or roadmap for the project. When the project is completed, read through these drafts once again and revise them to reflect what you have actually done before submitting your project for examination. That is, you must be sure that what is in the introduction is consistent with the various elements in the entire project.

The introduction is followed by the main body of the project, which will typically contain a number of chapters that discuss the methodology, the theory, the empirical aspects, as well as discussions and reflections as described in the following:

The Methodology Chapter

You will present your research design in this chapter. The research design explains the master plan of the research (i.e., how to conduct the research and the methods used). That is, you must specify which kinds of data you will collect, why, where, and how you will collect them, and how you will analyse the data in order to answer the research questions. (See chapter five of the book for a more detailed discussion. Additional information can be obtained in chapters eight, nine, and ten regarding choice of methods.)

The Theoretical Chapters

These are chapters that highlight your understanding of the existing body of theories on which your study is based. This may contain several chapters, depending on the nature of the project. (See chapter six of the book for a more detailed discussion.)

Empirical Chapters

These are chapters that present an analysis of the data as well as the major findings from the study. (See chapters eight, nine, and ten of the book for a more detailed discussion.)

Discussion and Reflection

You should devote a chapter to discussing the implications of your findings, as well as some reflections on the project process itself. This chapter allows you to take a final look at what you have done.

First, you will discuss the implications of your findings for the various stakeholders that the project concerns: governments, organisations, companies, and/or various groups in the society. Second, you will also reflect on how you have conducted the investigation, the difficulties that you have faced, and how you have addressed these difficulties. Third, you may specifically reflect on your choice of theories and method, noting the consistencies between them. (See chapter eleven of the book for a more detailed discussion.)

Summary and Conclusions

Following the main body of the project report, you write your summary and conclusions. Some students have a tendency to write their conclusions hurriedly as if they do not expect them to be read with any seriousness. You must pay attention to your conclusions. Most examiners will take a look at the introductory chapter of the project and then hold the contents against the conclusions in order to ascertain whether you have delivered what you promised in the introduction. That is, examiners read conclusions with substantial attention.

You may start your concluding chapter by briefly summarising the project, highlighting the main assumptions and findings. There must be consistency between what you have written in the introduction and the conclusion. That is, the conclusion must reflect the extent to which you have been successful in fulfilling the objectives set out for the project. Box 4.2 provides you with some guidelines on how to write conclusions.

Box 4.2. Guidelines for Writing Conclusion

- ▶ Are the conclusions related to the focus of the investigation (i.e., the research problem)?
- ▶ Do we have solid arguments and bring evidence to bear on the conclusions?
- ▶ What limitations does our analysis contain and how do these influence our conclusions?

References

References are very important. They establish the credibility of your arguments and indicate their main sources. Social science researchers have developed standard procedures for writing references. If your references deviate very much from the standard guidelines, this will reduce the quality of the project. This section of the chapter provides you with some guidelines on how to write references.

References can be classified into two types. There are citations in the text (or footnotes) and there is a list of references or biliography at the end of the project. Most universities recommend that students use the Harvard style citation. I have provided some examples of the Harvard style referencing below as a guide.

▶ If the article or book you are referencing is written by one author, you must list the author's name and the year of publication, as in the example below.

> Kuada (1994) suggests that culture impacts managerial behaviour.

▶ If you are quoting the exact words from the author, you must add the page on which the quote appears, as shown below:

> Kuada (1994:50) states that "an individual manager's behaviour will be determined by influences from his socio-cultural and organizational environment".

▶ If the reference is from two or three authors, you must write the last names of the all the authors followed by the year of publication, as shown in the example below:

> Kuada and Sørensen (2000) suggest that internationalization of firms can be viewed from both upstream and downstream perspectives.

▶ If the reference is from three or more authors, you write the last name of the first author followed by *et al* (in italics) and the year of publication. But you must remember to write the names of **all** the authors when preparing the list of references at the end of the report. See the example in the box below.

> Blumberg *et al.* (2005) provide a detailed discussion of mixed methods research.

You must present a list of all the references you have used in your project at the end of the report. The list must be presented in alphabetical order using the last names of the authors. The bibliography at the end of this book illustrates how to write your list of references.

Citing Sources from the Internet

There are no major differences between citing an Internet source and citing a book or a journal article, but you must remember to include the URL (the Web site address) at the end of the citation, followed by the date of access (i.e., the date you accessed the Internet source). It is advisable to copy and paste the URL to be sure that the address you have given is accurate. Most supervisors are uncomfortable with citations of documents for which no authors have been named. Please check with your supervisor if you intend to use such sources, and receive a clearance from him or her before you do so. Furthermore, some supervisors do not consider Wikipedia a reliable source that students can use. Again, check this with your supervisor.

DECIDING ON THE CONTENTS OF YOUR CHAPTERS AND PARAGRAPHS

The list of questions presented in box 4.3 can provide you with some guidelines on how to structure the chapters and paragraphs in your project.

> **Box 4.3. Guidelines for Structuring Chapters and Paragraphs**
>
> ▶ What kinds of information should we present in the chapter we are now writing?
> ▶ What is the relationship between this chapter and other chapters in the report?
> ▶ Have we drawn the reader's attention to the content and structure of the chapter?
> ▶ Can we justify the inclusion of the ideas and materials we are presenting (i.e., how detailed should the presentation be)?
> ▶ Has the central point come out clearly in our writing?
> ▶ Has the discussion in the chapter covered the mainstream viewpoints on the issue, or have we been too narrow in our selection of viewpoints?
> ▶ Are we critical enough in this presentation, or are we merely reproducing other peoples' viewpoints without a critical assessment of their relevance to the issues we are investigating?
> ▶ Have we made our personal standpoints on these issues clear enough in the paragraphs, sections, and the whole chapter?

KEY POINTS

This chapter highlights the importance of project structure. A well-structured project helps readers follow the arguments that students make and identifies the common thread that links the arguments and the logical progression of thoughts underlining them. A good structure also helps you remain focused throughout the writing process and therefore helps to save time. You must pay attention to the following:

- ▶ Spend sufficient time on planning the structure of the project.
- ▶ Be critical about what you write. The number of pages you write is not the main criterion for assessing the quality of your project.
- ▶ Always make sure that what you write contributes to addressing the research issues your project seeks to investigate.

PART 2
PROJECT DESIGN AND THEORETICAL PLATFORM

The research design is imperative to any academic research and, for that matter, a university student's project. It is the link between the research issues, the theories, the methods, and the results of the project. An important aspect of this link is the paradigmatic grounding of the project.

Part two introduces some of the key issues you must bear in mind when designing your project and choosing your theories and methods. It explains some of the fundamental concepts in the philosophy of science and how these concepts can guide you in making appropriate choices and adopting a scientific approach to your project. It consists of three chapters. Chapter five discusses how important research design is to your project. Chapter six informs you about the different types of theories in social science and the role of theories in your project. Chapter seven discusses metatheories, paradigms, and philosophy of science, and how they can help you write a good project.

CHAPTER 5
RESEARCH DESIGN

INTRODUCTION

Research design is the action plan or blueprint of your research. It should provide a logical sequence of activities that allows the reader of your project to see the connections between the research questions that you have posed in the introductory chapter of the project, the approach that you adopt to address the questions, the assumptions underlying your approach, how you collect and analyse your data, as well as your findings and conclusions. These choices require careful deliberation.

As we shall see in chapter seven, the metatheoretical (or paradigmatic) foundation of the project has a strong influence on the overall strategy of the project. But you are allowed to use whatever strategies, methods, or empirical materials at hand in order to fulfil the objectives of your investigations. That is, you can piece together and combine methods that serve your research purpose. The important thing for you to do is to explain what you have done and why you have made the various choices in your research design. You must also be aware of the limitations that various choices impose on your research, and discuss these limitations in your project.

This chapter draws attention to the fundamental concepts used in the literature to describe the issues that you should consider with regard to research design. It also provides you with guidelines on how to decide on an appropriate research approach.

THE FOUR LEVELS OF UNDERSTANDING

Most research methodology textbooks in social science identify four levels in a research design process. These levels feed into each other as illustrated in figure 5.1.

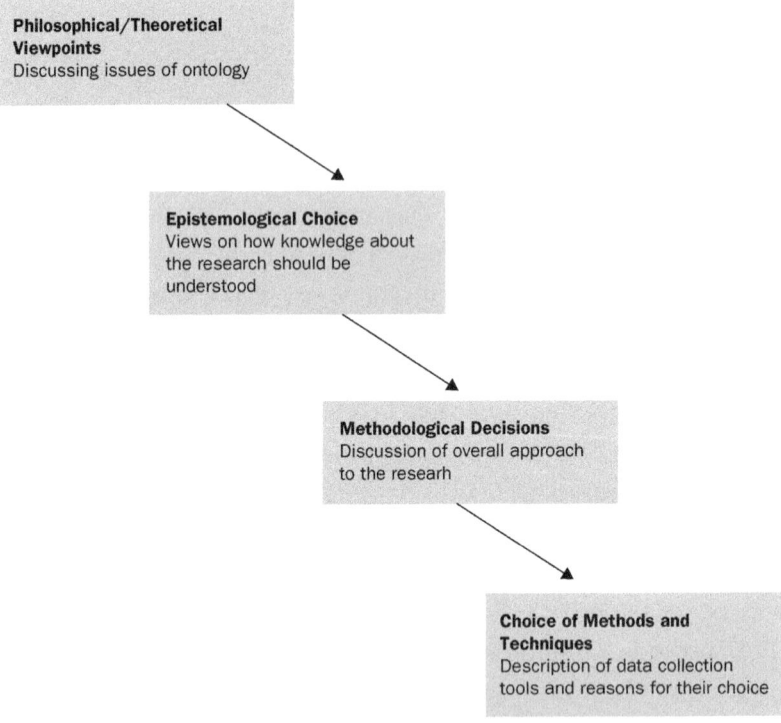

Fig. 5.1. Structure and Levels of Discussion in a Methodology Chapter

Level 1: The Philosophical and Theoretical Level

Ontology is a term used by philosophy of science scholars to describe the nature of what the researcher seeks to know (i.e., the "knowable" or "reality"). The social world that social science scholars investigate is usually seen from two broad perspectives. For some scholars the social world is real and external to an individual human being and therefore imposes itself on his or her consciousness. Other scholars hold the view that every individual creates his or her own social world. To these scholars the social world is subjectively constructed and therefore a product of human cognition.

Ontology also relates to how researchers see the relationship between human beings and their environment (i.e., a researcher's view of human nature). Some researchers see the social environment as being outside the individual. Other researchers hold the view that human beings and the social environment codetermine each other.

In sum, assumptions that you make about human beings and the environment will define your perception of reality. This perception, in turn, underlies what you will consider as a *truth* and how knowledge about this *truth* should be acquired.

Level 2: Epistemological Level

Epistemology is a term that describes the nature of knowledge and the means of knowing (i.e., "how we know what we know" or what we conceive as a truth). Some scholars hold the view that it is possible (as external observers) to know the truth about a specific social world. Others maintain that the social world can only be understood by occupying the frame of reference of the individual actor whom the researcher seeks to study; that is, the social world must be studied intersubjectively.

Level 3: Methodological Approach

Methodology describes the reasons underlying the choice and use of specific methods in the research process (i.e., how you may go about gaining the knowledge you desire). If you assume that the social world can be objectively observed from outside, you will adopt a methodology that focuses on an examination of relationships, but if you assume that the social world can only be understood by obtaining first-hand knowledge of the persons under investigation, you will opt for a methodology that focuses on individuals' interpretations of the world as they experience it.

Level 4: Methods and Techniques

This level requires you to describe the specific data collection methods and techniques you adopt in your study. You must also inform your readers about the problems you faced in the data collection process and how you solved these problems. For example, if you choose to conduct interviews, you must indicate what interviewing techniques you have used and in what sort of setting the interviews have been conducted. You must also show the link between the methods selected and the problem formulation, as well as the consistency between the methods and the three levels of understanding described above (i.e., the ontological perspectives, the epistemological considerations, and the methodological approaches) (see Crotty, 1998 for elaboration).

EXCLUSIVE VERSUS COMPLEMENTARY APPROACHES

There is a controversy in the research methodology literature as to whether researchers can see reality only from an objective (i.e., external) or subjective (i.e., socially constructed) perspective, or whether reality can be seen from both perspectives in the same project. In other words, should researchers consider the two views of reality as mutually exclusive (i.e., they cannot be combined) or should researchers see them as complementary (i.e., their combinations are useful and insightful)? As indicated above, the way you view reality will influence other aspects of your research design.

Following Rossman and Wilson (1985), researchers can be grouped into three categories, depending on their views on reality. One category of researchers holds the view that the objective and subjective perspectives on reality are mutually exclusive. In other words, the root assumptions on which each of the two perspectives is grounded are very different and must not be blended. Researchers adopting this viewpoint are labelled *purists* in the literature.

Another category of researchers adopt a flexible attitude to the two perspectives. These researchers argue that all social phenomena have many sides and interpretations. It is therefore useful to combine both objective and subjective perspectives on reality in a single research project in order to gain a deeper insight into the research issue that is being studied. In other words, the objective and subjective perspectives are best seen as points on a continuum rather than as alternative perspectives. But the degree of emphasis on objective or subjective dimensions of reality must depend on every research situation. In some research situations, researchers may lean more toward objectivist views of reality; in some situations, the subjective views may be preferable; and in other situations, some combination of objectivist and subjectivist views of reality may be appropriate. Researchers endorsing this view are labelled *situationalists* in the literature.

The third category of researchers holds the view that the nature of research issues and the objectives of an investigation should determine the view of reality that a researcher adopts. These researchers are labelled *pragmatists*. They neither accept nor reject the notion that the two perspectives on reality can be combined or used separately. They simply say that the nature of the research task rather than the research situation must decide what view of reality you may consider to be appropriate. Some tasks are suitable for an objectivist view of reality while other tasks may be suitable for a subjectivist view. If your problem formulation shows that an objective or a subjective perspective of reality is appropriate, you must make a choice. Furthermore, you may also combine two or more views of reality in a single project if the problem formulation shows that a combination of views is appropriate in providing the best insight.

One can say that there are simply nuanced differences between the situationalist and the pragmatist researcher, but while the situationalist may be more inclined to use a combination of perspectives in a given project, the pragmatist is more likely to select one perspective (without rejecting a combined approach). The purist, on the other hand, rejects combinations under all circumstances.

The discussions above suggest that you need to state explicitly if your understanding of reality (and how to apply it in research) follows the views of a purist, a situationalist, or a pragmatist. You must also provide arguments that justify your views and discuss them with your supervisor.

KEY POINTS

This chapter emphasises the need for you to develop a comprehensive strategy for your research. The results you obtain from your investigations will depend on your views on the following four issues:

▶ How reality must be perceived (i.e., objective or subjective, or a combination of both)
▶ How you should go about acquiring knowledge about that reality
▶ Whether you are interested in finding universal truths in your study or seeking to gain unique understanding and interpretations of the social reality you investigate
▶ The specific methods and techniques you adopt to gain that knowledge

You need to reflect upon and discuss which of these views you subscribe to and how your choices will influence the results of your study.

CHAPTER 6
THE ROLE OF THEORIES IN YOUR PROJECT

INTRODUCTION

An important requirement in your project work is that you must demonstrate a good understanding of what other people have written about the issues central to your own investigation; that is, your project must be grounded in existing knowledge about your subject. To do so, you need to review the existing literature that is relevant to your problem statements. The literature review forms the theoretical foundation of your study.

Some students find this literature review to be unnecessary, particularly if they are much more interested in solving what they consider to be mainly a practical business, social, or institutional problem. It is true that your future employers will be much more interested in practical and workable solutions to the problems that you face at work, but the PBL approach to education is that good knowledge of the existing theories in a particular field of study will improve students' understanding and analysis of the specific issues that they will be confronted with in real-life situations.

The aim of this chapter is therefore to emphasise the importance of theories and to draw your attention to the various types of theories that exist in the social science literature. It also discusses the roles that theories play in solving social science problems and provides you with some guidelines on how to conduct your literature review.

WHAT IS A THEORY?

The meaning of the word *theory* varies with the context in which it is used. In social science, theories may be defined as series of systematic inter-related statements or generalisations that explain and/or anticipate developments in a specific context or phenomenon. Strauss and Corbin (1998:15) define theory as "a set of well-developed concepts related through statements of relationship which together constitute an integrated framework that can be used to explain or predict phenomena".

Thus, theory provides the language, the concepts, and assumptions that help researchers to make sense of the phenomenon that they seek to investigate. It enables researchers to connect the issues they are investigating to the existing body of knowledge in the area.

CLASSIFICATION OF THEORIES

There are different classifications of theories in the social science literature. One of the well-known classifications identifies the following four levels of theory:

- Metatheories
- Grand theories
- Midrange theories
- Microtheories

Metatheories describe the broad philosophical assumptions concerning reality that are accepted in social science as clearly demarcated boundaries of thought in a particular field of study. An adoption of a metatheoretical position in particular research therefore implies commitment of the researcher to conceptual assumptions underlying that metatheory. For example, cultural studies are usually based on different metatheoretical assumptions. Some scholars conceive culture as a component of a social system aimed at fulfilling specific social functions (i.e., a functionalist perspective of culture); others see it as a product of historical evolution (i.e., social diffusionist perspective); yet others see it as an outcome of human cognition (i.e., ideational perspective). See Allaire and Firsirotu (1984) for an elaboration.

As indicated in chapter five, these assumptions are embedded in the ontological, epistemological, and methodological views of the researcher. In other words, metatheories serve the following purposes:

1. clarifying the general assumptions underlying a subject matter;
2. specifying the important problems faced in undertaking investigations;
3. and specifying what are acceptable methods.

The concept of metatheories is frequently used interchangeably with the concept of paradigm (see chapter seven).

A *grand theory* is defined as an all-inclusive unified theory that seeks to explain social behaviour, social organization, and social change in human experience. It normally provides the key concepts and principles of the social science discipline and is therefore consistent with the dominant metatheories or paradigms of the discipline. For example, grand theory in economics defines the laws of scarcity and needs as well as the relationship between demand, supply, and pricing. Feminism, marxism, and democracy are also grand theories in political science with crossdisciplinary implications for other social science disciplines.

Grand theories may also be found in specific fields of study. For example, one grand theory in cultural studies is that there are universally identifiable dimensions of culture that can be found in all societies and groups. Cultures can therefore be compared on the basis of these universal dimensions and the manner in which they evolve over time in the history of a society (see Hofstede, 2001). An alternative grand theory is that culture is socially constructed and continuously negotiated among groups of people. As such it cannot be studied by using universal dimensions (see Gullestrup, 2006).

Midrange theory is a term that emerged in sociological studies in the 1940s (frequently associated with the work of Robert K. Merton). It represents theories that connect grand theories with empirical evidence. It consists of limited sets of assumptions from which specific hypotheses are logically derived and confirmed by empirical investigation (see Merton, 1968). Thus, when you engage in literature review, you are mostly discussing midrange theories. For example, if you adopt a universalist approach to cultural studies, you will review the works of scholars that have adopted this approach in specific empirical investigations and use their findings to justify your hypothesis formulation. Similarly, if you adopt a social constructivist approach to your cultural research, you will justify your arguments by using studies that have adopted this approach.

As students you can aspire to develop midrange theories, as a way of providing general statements from your empirical investigations, if your research design enables you to do so. In doing so you will be contributing to the extension of the existing boundaries of your specific fields of research and at the same time deepening your understandings of the core content of the subjects that you are studying.

Microtheories constitute the lowest level of theories. They focus on individuals or small groups located in specific contexts. As such explanations found in microtheories are of limited generalization on their own. They can, however, constitute essential inputs in the generation of new perspectives and theory development. Some scholars use case studies to generate microtheories that are then further developed through multiple case studies to become important inputs in midrange theory formulation.

Again, continuing with the example with cultural studies, you may undertake an investigation of the culture of a sports organisation (e.g., a football club) in a particular community. You may gain a good understanding of how the culture of that club has developed over time and how it has influenced the accepted rules of behaviour in the club. Though this investigation cannot be generalized across all football clubs in a particular country, it can produce useful inputs into how football clubs in small communities may be investigated.

Your awareness of the differences in the levels of theory informs your readers that you understand the nuances in the research you are doing. This also helps in positioning your own work within the existing body of work in the field.

USE OF THEORIES

Theories are found in the literature that you read. Each of the levels of theory listed above will play a different role in your project. The metatheories define the philosophical foundations of your project (i.e., paradigms as discussed in chapter seven). The grand theories define the boundaries of your subject of investigation. They combine with the metatheories to establish the platform on which you will base your research. But much of the discussion in your theoretical chapters will draw on midrange theories. Through studying previous work done on your topic, you will become acquainted with the mainstream concepts used in the literature to describe your problem and its constituent elements. Thus, when you do your literature review you are mostly engaged in a discussion of midrange theories.

Midrange theories can also be used to develop variables to analyse and the connections between them: an *analytical framework*. They therefore help you identify what kind of information you require for the analysis and what is the most appropriate means of acquiring this information. Without such an analytical framework you will risk drowning in a sea of information, since you will be unable to sort out the relevant from the irrelevant.

There are, however, many competing theories within each subject area. An essential task in the project work process is for you to discuss most of the leading theories that attempt to explain the problem of interest, comparing the strengths of the arguments underlying them and their empirical foundation. In this process of discussion, it is important to draw on the views of other writers in the field who have undertaken similar investigations. Such discussions will sharpen your understanding of the theories as well as their limitations in explaining the problems you are investigating.

All the theories that you use in your research need not be discussed in a single chapter. If you decide to use multiple sets of theories, each set can be discussed in a separate chapter. You can then write another separate chapter to synthesise the discussions in the preceeding theoretical chapters and use this chapter to present your overall analytical framework for the project.

GUIDELINES FOR LITERATURE REVIEW

It is important for you to read the most recent literature that reflects the most recent knowledge on the topic you choose to write on. It is also important to read published studies in journals in addition to textbooks. Box 6.1 provides a list of questions that can guide you in your review of the existing literature.

> **Box 6.1. Guidelines for Literature Review**
>
> ▶ What are the main concepts and ideas in the book or article that I have read?
> ▶ Do the author's ideas agree with or corroborate ideas I have come across in other articles or books? Or do the ideas differ from them? What are the points of agreement and/or differences?
> ▶ How do I explain the differences in the viewpoints?
> ▶ Is there any agreement among the authors on the definition of concepts and angles of perception?
> ▶ Which of these concepts, ideas, and conclusions do I find relevant to our own work and why?

In reviewing the literature, three main factors need to be carefully examined:

- The date of publication and the years in which the researcher has collected the data used.
- The country in which the study has been conducted (if it is an empirical piece of work).
- The metatheoretical approach adopted by the researcher and the data collection methods used (see chapter seven for elaboration).

Remember that what you read in previous studies is usually a snapshot of the phenomenon that other researchers have investigated—in other words, what they have found in a given context and at a given point in time. Since you are likely to use the knowledge in that study within a different timeframe, it is important for you to examine the validity and relevance of the knowledge at the time of the publication of the article or book that you have read.

The research setting (i.e., the country where the writer collected his or her data) is also important to note since it provides an idea about the context of the knowledge presented. For example, a study done about export promotion in an African country may not reflect requirements for export sector development in Denmark.

KEY POINTS

The theory chapters in your project are essential. They serve the following purposes:

- They demonstrate your understanding of the current body of knowledge in your chosen field of study.
- They provide you with a philosophical foundation on which you can ground your study.
- They constitute an important part of the overall research design of the project.

Remember that there are different levels of theory in the literature. This chapter has drawn your attention to metatheories, grand theories, midrange theories, and microtheories. These levels of theory play different roles in your study.

CHAPTER 7
METATHEORIES, PARADIGMS, AND PHILOSOPHY OF SCIENCE

INTRODUCTION

Philosophy of science scholars have argued that whether or not a researcher is aware of it, and whether or not assumptions are stated, the choice of research questions and the presumed adequacy of research methods in addressing such questions conveys an adherence to fundamental prior assumptions relating to ontology, epistemology, views on human nature, and methodology (see chapter five). Researchers that explicitly articulate these assumptions help themselves in reflecting on their work and help their readers to make better sense of it. The concept of paradigm is now accepted in the philosophy of science literature as providing a summary description of these assumptions. Thus, the concept of paradigm is often used interchangeably with metatheory.

The aim of this chapter is to provide you with an overview of some of the most widely adopted classifications of paradigms. They should help you to understand assumptions underlying the arguments in the research papers and books that you read in connection with your project. They also provide you with inspirations for developing your own assumptions. In this way you will be able to ground your own study on solid philosophical foundations, by building on established academic traditions and thoughts.

THE CONCEPT OF PARADIGM

In its modern usage, the term *paradigm* is attributed to Kuhn (1970) who presented a theory of the structure of scientific revolutions to describe waves of research in a given scientific field. Kuhn argues that every field of research is characterised by a set of common understandings of what kind of phenomenon is being studied, the kinds of questions that are useful to ask about the phenomenon, how researchers should structure their approach to answering their research questions, and how the results should be interpreted. These common characteristics constitute a paradigm. He argues further that science does not progress only from a gradual accumulation of facts, but also by successive waves of thought that fundamentally reframe ideas. These ideas may be overlapping in the short run, but over time they tend to alter the nature of what researchers take to be facts. As previously stated, most scholars of philosophy of science define paradigms in terms of four sets of assumptions: ontological, epistemological, methodological, and assumptions about human nature (see chapter five).

OBJECTIVE-SUBJECTIVE PERSPECTIVES IN SOCIAL SCIENCE

The discussions of paradigms in social science have been influenced by a general distinction between *objective* and *subjective* approaches to research, which Andersen (1990) sees as two polar perspectives. He labels them as the *positivistic paradigm* and the *interpretive paradigm*, respectively. Burrell and Morgan (1979) compare the two divergent perspectives in terms of their ontology, epistemology, human nature, and methodology. The differences are presented in figure 7.1.

DIMENSIONS	THE OBJECTIVIST APPROACH	THE SUBJECTIVIST APPROACH
Ontology	Realism	Nominalism
Epistemology	Positivism	Antipositivism
Human Nature	Determinism	Voluntarism
Methodology	Nomothetic	Idiographic

Fig. 7.1. The Objectivist-Subjectivist Dispositions in Social Science

Following Fast and Clark (1998), *realism* postulates that the social world is real and external to individual cognition; that is, the world is made up of hard, tangible, and relatively immutable structures. *Nominalism*, on the other hand, assumes that reality is constructed by individuals in interaction with each other and is presented in the form of names, labels, and concepts. One can therefore speak of multiple realities in social science.

Positivism reflects an epistemology that seeks to explain and predict what happens in the social world with an emphasis on regularities and causal relationships between its constituent elements. The positivist researcher believes that any social science researcher can be objective and conduct his or her investigations as an external observer. He or she can therefore study the constituent parts of a social phenomenon in order to understand the whole; that is, the positivist looks for regularities and causal relationships to understand and predict the social world.

Antipositivism, on the other hand, takes various forms but mostly assumes that the social world is essentially relativistic (e.g., socially constructed) and can only be understood from the standpoint of individuals directly involved in the social activities under investigation. Scholars adopting this viewpoint are uncomfortable with the notion that social science research can generate objective knowledge of any kind.

While the *nomothetic* approach encourages studies that are based on systematic protocol and techniques such as survey methods, the *ideographic* approach sees reality in terms of symbols and ideas. Scholars adopting the latter approach therefore emphasise analyses of the everyday flow of life of those investigated. This is a kind of anthropological approach, or an action research, through which the researcher "gets inside" the situation by getting close to the people he or she is studying and by allowing them to tell their own stories rather than responding to predefined questions. This approach therefore endorses the use of such techniques as diaries, biographies, and participant-observations.

Many methodology textbooks describe the objectivist types of research with the label *positivism* and the subjectivist research is labelled *interpretivism*. As indicated above, the positivist paradigm assumes that all social phenomena can be explained by observing their causes and effects. This implies that existing theories can form the bases for hypotheses that provide a priori explanations for a given social phenomenon. These hypotheses can then be tested to verify or falsify the theories. This approach is generally referred to in the literature as the *hypothetico-deductive* method. Interpretivism takes an opposite viewpoint. It subscribes to understanding a given social world from the points of view of people being studied and the intentions underlying their behaviour. It therefore uses the inductive method, basing conclusions on specific observations rather than logical arguments that may not necessarily be supported by empirical evidence.

But not all researchers consider this classification to be very useful. For example, Deetz (1996) argues that the meaning of the objective-subjective labels is socially contrived and the *objective* practices are, in a sense, the most *subjective* forms of research. His reasoning is that in objective research, concepts and methods are held a priori and constitute projections of a researcher's own ways of encountering the world. In other words, the researcher does not engage in any critical reflection over his or her work process and does not contemplate possible alternative perspectives on the social world that he or she seeks to understand.

CLASSIFICATIONS OF PARADIGMS IN SOCIAL SCIENCE

The objective-subjective debate has produced a number of typologies of paradigms. Three of the most popular typologies are presented in this chapter. Two factors have influenced this selection. First, the three classifications are those commonly found in the social science methodology textbooks used in Scandinavian colleges and universities. Second, all the classifications have strong roots in classical sociological studies. They are:

▶ the FISI classification (covering functionalism, interpretivism, structuralism, and interactionism);
▶ the RRIF classification (covering radical humanism, radical structuralism, interpretivism, and functionalism),
▶ and Abnor and Bjerke's classification of six paradigms and three research approaches.

Each of the paradigms described in the chapter considers some research issues to be more important than others; thus, your choice of paradigm will influence how you define and explain research issues in your project. In other words, as you read the root assumptions underlying these paradigms, reflect on how they relate to the assumptions of the theories you intend to use in your project. Such reflections will improve your understanding of the theories. As you reflect on these theories, you must examine the degrees of consistency between your own assumptions and those held by the authors of the theories. Where discrepancies are noted, you must discuss the implications of such discrepancies for your investigations.

The FISI Classification

Scholars of sociology in the nineteenth and early mid-twentieth centuries (e.g., Emile Durkheim, Herbert Spencer, Talcott Parsons, and Robert Merton) have emphasised the importance of studying social phenomena in terms of structures, functions, and interactions. In general, these scholars argue that social facts have existences outside individual actions. As such, they can be studied with positivist epistemology and its associated methodological arrangements. The FISI classification of paradigms (see figure 7.2) provides a simple classification of the root assumptions of their work.

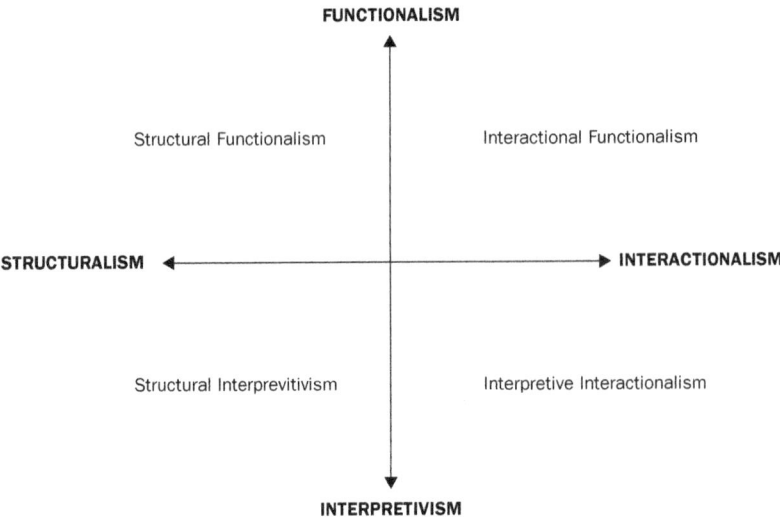

Fig. 7.2. FISI Classification of Paradigms

Functionalism subscribes to a positivist epistemology. It therefore falls under the objectivist or positivist types of research. It is popular in some strands of social science research, including economics and its derived disciplines. Business economists adopting the functionalist paradigm hold the view that organisations make adaptive structural changes in order to align themselves with their operational environment. A classical example of this viewpoint is found in the stimulus-organism-response (SOR) model in business economics. This model argues that environmental factors stimulate organisations, which in turn respond to the environmental stimulus with specific behaviours (including strategies). In other words, organisations are likened to simple biological organisms whose response behaviours are determined by factors within the environments in which they live.

Recent organisational studies have, however, acknowledged limitations to ultrafunctionalist views of business. An increasing number of scholars now agree that changes in strategy and structure occur because of decisions by managers whose decision-making processes may involve many subjective elements, including perceptions and beliefs (Donaldson, 1997). Grant and Perren (2002) therefore suggest that advances in business research require a broadening of perspectives, new understandings, and theories.

Interpretivism emphasises the need to understand how people define situations in which they are involved and the meanings they derive from their experiences. While functionalists are preoccupied with explaining events or experiences as objective evidence separate from those experiencing them, and often without direct reference to the contextual setting, an interpretive paradigm requires investigators to perceive their actors as engaged in continuous interpretation, meaning creation and sense-making of events and their contexts. Investigators therefore focus their work on understanding rather than explaining. These investigators subscribe to the view that human beings do not passively respond to what is going on around them.

Structuralism (as an approach to social science) sees human societies as composed of complex systems of interrelated parts. A notable characteristic of the structuralist perspective is an emphasis on the collective rather than the individual. The individual's position within a social system is defined by the structure of the system. There is therefore some element of determinism in this perspective. Examples of the structuralist approach in business studies can be found in the analysis of organisational structures and behaviours. Variables such as size, type of industry, number of competitors, and number of buyers and sellers occupy central positions in such analyses. A close relationship is seen between structures and sizes of organisations (Chandler, 1962). The structure-conduct-performance (SCP) model is one of the well-known models in business studies that exemplifies this approach.

Interactionist approaches to social knowledge emphasise the role of human interactions in the functioning of social life. The understanding among these scholars is that individuals do not simply respond to stimuli in the environment in pre-established ways, but instead construct their acts through "minded behaviour", which involves the presentation of oneself with anticipated and alternative possibilities of future action (Meltzer, 2003).

Social interactions allow individuals to share meanings and expectations, reflect over events via cognitive interactions with themselves, and act with one another on the basis of shared meanings and understandings; thus, interactions are at the centre of all social acts and facts. The best-known proponents of the interactionist perspective in social science are scholars who subscribe to a social constructivist perspective on understanding social worlds. This perspective emphasises the view that people consistently engage in the creation and sharing of meanings through their interactions with each other. These meanings are therefore essentially subjective.

There are various combinations of the four paradigms presented above. The best known among them are the following:

▶ Structural functionalism
▶ Structural interpretivism
▶ Interactional functionalism
▶ Interpretive interactionalism

Structural functionalism is a spin-off from both structuralism and functionalism and aims at transcending the dichotomies of both epistemological perspectives. The general understanding among the proponents of this paradigm is that society has an existence over and above individuals. In Parson's (1951) formulation, structural functionalism describes four characteristics of social systems:

▶ *Adaptation*: Capacity to interact with and adjust to external contexts. This is evident in technological adaptations in modern societies.
▶ *Goal-attainment*: Capability of social systems to set goals and im-

plement appropriate decisions. This is found in modern organisational forms and political systems.
- *Integration*: Capability to create harmony and convergence through shared values and norms. This is found in social networks and civil societal structures.
- *Latency*: Capability to establish stable pattern over time through socialisation of new members into existing norms and values. This is found in well-functioning schools and family systems in modern societies.

Structural interpretivists endorse the view that the social world is organised in terms of some basic structures that define relationships, but they emphasise the interpretations that individuals accord events and experiences within the structures rather than the structures themselves. That is, scholars adopting the structural interpretivist perspective view reality as providing shifting frames of reference for individual actions. They therefore seek to understand the social world through the eyes of individuals. Because they believe that reality can only be revealed by those engaged in the experience, they use methods that can capture subjective experiences of the individual participants within defined structures.

Interactional functionalism combines functionalism and interactionism. As noted earlier, scholars adopting the functionalist perspective also believe that social institutions are made up of interconnected roles or inter-related norms; thus, interactions are essential for the effective functioning of social systems. Interactions produce social norms and the predictability of behaviours that allow expectations to be built and roles to be defined. Scholars adopting this perspective see roles in societies (and groups) as normatively regulated behaviours that emerge through social interactions. Interactions create history and norms that influence current and future behaviours. Individuals and organisations are thus believed to be held partly captive by their histories. This understanding is reflected, for example, in *path dependence* theories in business research. Path dependence explains how the set of decisions one faces for any given circumstance is limited by the decisions one has made in the past, even though past circumstances may no longer be relevant, a phenomenon described by Cyert and March (1963) as the "competence trap".

Interpretive interactionalists who study organisations and institutions hold the view that individual members of organisations and their communities interact within and outside their organisational boundaries. As they do so they use their cognitive faculties and memories to interpret events. It is the process of interacting and interpreting that defines their behaviours. As such, individual decisions are not totally deterministic or responses to an objective environment. The interpretivists therefore adopt the concept of "enacted" environment in explaining organizational decisions and strategies, drawing on the studies in sociology (Weber, 1968), symbolic interactionism (Blumer, 1969), the sociology of knowledge (Berger and Luckmann, 1967), as well as cognitive social psychology. The argument here is that environments are enacted through interactions with other actors within the environment and a sense-making process through which individuals assign and read meanings into the environment that they co-create with others.

The various combinations of paradigms presented within the FISI typology hints at the willingness of social scientists to allow for multiple paradigmatic perspectives in social science research. This issue is discussed more comprehensively in chapter seven.

The RRIF Classification of Burrell and Morgan

Another classification system is that provided by Burrell and Morgan (1979). Their classification has become very influential in organisational studies, though scholars in other social science disciplines have also found it highly useful. The classification and its underlying arguments are presented here for a quick overview. Burrell and Morgan drew a distinction between what they called the "sociology of regulation" and the "sociology of radical change". They used the term *sociology of regulation* to describe those approaches to sociology that concentrate on explaining the nature of social order and equilibrium. *Sociology of radical change* describes those studies in sociology that are concerned with the problems of change, conflict, and coercion within human social units. The radical change paradigm borrows from thoughts found in critical social research inspired by the writings of such scholars as Karl Marx, Max Weber, Antonio Gramsci, Jurgen Habermas, Pierre Bourdieu, and Michel Foucault. Critical theories draw attention to inequalities, malpractice, injustice, and exploitation in social worlds, and seek to give voice to marginalised groups. The inclusion of critical perspectives allows Burrell and Morgan to contrast functionalist and interpretive paradigms with the "radical" humanist and structuralist paradigms to produce four paradigms for organizational analysis, thereby extending traditional classifications of paradigms in social science.

As shown in figure 7. 3, the four paradigms are:

▶ The functionalist paradigm
▶ The interpretive paradigm
▶ The radical humanist paradigm
▶ The radical structuralist paradigm

In presenting this typology, the authors argue that these paradigms should be considered "contiguous but separate—contiguous because of the shared characteristics, but separate because the differentiation is . . . of sufficient importance to warrant treatment of the paradigms as four distinct entities" (Burrell and Morgan, 1979: 23). As such, the four paradigms provide fundamentally different perspectives for the analysis of social phenomena, including organisations.

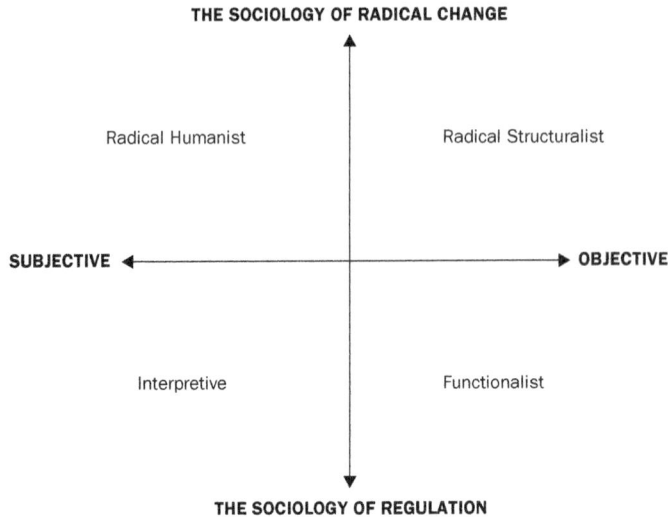

Fig. 7.3. Burrell and Morgan's Four Paradigms Model of Social Theory (Source: Adapted from Burrell and Morgan (1979))

Again, the *functionalist paradigm* (objective regulation) in Burrell and Morgan's typology is the combination of objectivity and order. It rests upon the premise that society has a real, concrete existence and a systematic character, and is directed toward the production of order and regulation. From this perspective, social issues can be assumed to be objective and value free. The researcher can therefore distance himself or herself from the subject matter by the rigour of the scientific method that he or she adopts.

Burrell and Morgan also present the *interpretive paradigm* as rejecting the analysis of structures "independent of the minds of men" (p. 260). That is, scholars adopting the interpretive paradigm will invariably be highly subjective and qualitative in their studies. These scholars are likely to view social events as occurring in complex, ambiguous, and ill-defined contexts. In other words, if you adopt an interpretive paradigm as a philosophical foundation for your study you will be concerned primarily with the experiences of the individuals you study rather than the outcomes of the decisions they make or the actions they take.

The *radical humanist paradigm* (subjective-radical change) shares with the interpretive paradigm the assumption that everyday reality is socially constructed. Scholars adopting this approach see the dynamics of social change process in terms of interactions between individual worldviews and the external institutionalised world in which they live. The external world is often so powerful that social change requires the emancipation of the consciousness of individual participants within the society. This understanding is at the root of missionary endeavours. The activities of high profile not-for-profit organisations such as Greenpeace and Amnesty International are examples of institutions with radical humanist orientations.

Scholars subscribing to the *radical structuralist paradigm* (objective-radical change) see inherent structural conflicts within society. These conflicts generate constant change through political and economic crises. This has been the fundamental paradigm of scholars such as Marx and Engles, and of politicians such as Lenin of Russia and Mao of China.

Burrell and Morgan's introduction of the sociology of radical change in their classification of paradigms differentiates their classification from the FISI classification presented above. Radical changes have been presented and advocated for in political sociology but have gained little acknowledgement in disciplines that have developed in the market-driven societies.

Burrell and Morgan's classification has also been criticised by several authors. Some argue that the four-paradigm classification has often led to quick categorizations and to debates about the appropriateness of different paradigms for different types of studies. Deetz (1996) aptly argues, however, that one should not use the four categories as simply means of positioning one's work or the work of others. The focus of the research (i.e., the problem formulation) should determine which of the four paradigms the researcher may consider to be appropriate for the investigation. It is also useful to consider whether the focal research issue can allow for a combination of paradigms, granting that such a combination produces richer insights into the phenomenon.

Others point out that the model is based on dualisms. As such it fails to recognise both the existence of continua and the dialectical nature of these characteristics. As Deetz (1996) argues, it is intellectually appropriate to see subjectivity and objectivity as mutually constitutive, each implying the other. In this sense subjectivism and objectivism complement each other.

Abnor and Bjerke's Three Methodological Approaches

A third and more recent typology of paradigms is offered by Abnor and Bjerke (2009). Consistent with previous definitions, Abnor and Bjerke draw a distinction between the theory of science and methods. To them the theory of science covers the ultimate presumptions (or ontological and epistemological discourses) in the social sciences. They also draw a distinction between paradigms and methodological approaches. In their view, paradigms describe the relation between the ultimate presumptions of the researcher and the practical use of various methodological approaches. A methodological approach clarifies the ultimate presumptions as they relate to the specific study and at the same time sets up a framework for a more concrete approach to the study.

Arbnor and Bjerke suggest the following six overlapping paradigms:

- Reality as a concrete phenomenon that conforms to law and is independent of the observer (O1)
- Reality as a concrete determining process (O2)
- Reality as mutually dependent fields of information (O3)
- Reality as a world of symbolic discourse (SO1)
- Reality as a social construction (S1)
- Reality as a manifestation of human intentionality (S2)

Based on these six paradigms, they identified three methodological approaches that researchers use for creating knowledge (see fig. 7.5):

▶ The analytical approach
▶ The systems approach
▶ The actors approach

The *analytical approach* is characterized by the belief that reality is objective and independent of the observer. Objective reality is, in this regard, assumed to have a summative character, implying that the whole is the sum of its parts. Researchers can thus decompose an objective phenomenon that they investigate into its constituent parts and analyse each part separately. They can then bring them together to build a total picture.

Epistemologically, the ultimate presumption underlying an analytical approach is that knowledge is based on facts. The researcher can therefore adopt a neutral position in the study and distance himself or herself from the respondents. In this way knowledge is independent of the individual's subjective experience and can be generated by formal logic. Abnor and Bjerke's analytical approach is similar to the functionalist paradigm identified in the other typologies introduced above. Figure 7.4 provides a summary of the three ontological perspectives that underlie the analytical approach.

DIMENSIONS	Paradigm 01	Paradigm 02	Paradigm 03
ONTOLOGY	Reality as concrete phenomenon that is conformable to law and independent of the observer	Reality as a concrete determining process	Reality as mutually dependent fields of information
RESEARCH APPROACH HUMAN NATURE METHODOLOGY		Analytical Approach	

Fig. 7.4. Ontological Considerations in the Analytical Approach

Note that in the figure the paradigms O1, O2, and O3 stand for the relative positions of the objective paradigms on the objective-subjective continuum. In other words, you should read the figure as follows:

▶ Paradigm O1 represents the extreme objectivist position
▶ Paradigm O2 represents the second objectivist position on the continuum
▶ Paradigm O3 represents the third objectivist position on the continuum

In a *systems approach*, a social entity such as a group, an organization, or a community is conceived as a system consisting of constituent elements. Between these elements relations exist. These relations can reflect the synergistic properties within an existing system. Within a system various subsystems may be distinguished. Each system has its specific characteristics, in terms of its constituent elements as well as its mutual relations. Researchers seek to find out how changes in one constituent element may change the other elements in the system.

The systems approach in Abnor and Bjerke's methodology thus assumes the existence of an objective (or at least objectively accessible) reality that researchers consider to be their primary field of interest. It allows the researcher to focus his or her study on one or a combination of the following two issues:

▶ Static structures of the system
▶ Regular and nonregular processes.

Static structures are the fixed, stable characteristics in a social system. Processes, on the other hand, draw attention to the mechanisms that produce changes within the system and the patterns of changes that take place. The *regular processes* are those changes that are dynamic but evolutionary, while the *nonregular processes* refer to radical departures from existing patterns of thinking and behaviour that may bring about total and swift changes within the system. Under conditions of radical change, knowledge is valid only for a short span of time and must therefore be subject to constant revision. Unlike the analytical approach that makes an implicit assumption of the environment as being stable and therefore highly predictable, the systems approach draws attention to the possible unpredictability of the context within which social actors are located. Figure 7.5 provides a summary of the three ontological perspectives that underlie the systems approach.

DIMENSIONS	Paradigm O2	Paradigm O3	Paradigm SO1
ONTOLOGY	Reality as a concrete determining process	Reality as mutually dependent fields of information	Reality as a world of symbolic discourse
RESEARCH APPROACH HUMAN NATURE METHODOLOGY		Systems Approach	

Fig. 7.5. Ontological Considerations in the Systems Approach

Note that again the paradigms O2, O3, and SO1 stand for the relative positions of the objective paradigms on the objective-subjective continuum. I have used "SO" to illustrate a middle position in the continuum reflecting some degree of subjective and objective dimensions. In other words, you should read the figure as follows:

▶ Paradigm O2 represents the second position on the objective-subjective continuum (as shown in fig. 7.4).
▶ Paradigm O3 represents the third position on the objective-subjective continuum.
▶ Paradigm SO1 represents the fourth position on the objective-subjective continuum. It combines some degrees of objectivism and subjectivism.

For Abnor and Bjerke, the *actors approach* differs very much from the previous two approaches outlined above. Researchers subscribing to this approach see reality as emerging from interactions between each individual's own experiences and the experiences of others within his or her social community over a period of time. In other words, reality is socially constructed through continuous negotiations and sharing of meaning; thus, the approach emphasises concepts such as subjectivity, individuality, and interaction. As social actors act, their actions produce results over which they may reflect and which guide their subsequent actions. Actions, counteractions, reflections, and thoughts in turn combine to influence the ongoing process of their social development. In Abnor and Bjerke's view, reality is regarded in the actor approach as consisting of a number of "finite provinces of meaning" that are shared by a larger or smaller number of people.

The actors approach has methodological similarities with those suggested for the interpretive paradigm in Burrell and Morgan's taxonomy. Scholars seeing the world from an actor's perspective will feel at home with such research methods as hermeneutics and symbolic analysis (symbolic interactionism). Dialogue constitutes an important tool in this approach as well and is characterised by the interplay between "talking" and "listening" that takes place on equal terms for the participants. Figure 7.6 provides a summary of the ontological considerations in the actors approach.

DIMENSIONS	Paradigm SO1	Paradigm S1	Paradigm S2
ONTOLOGY	Reality as a world of symbolic discourse	Reality as social construction	Reality as a manifestation of human intentionality
RESEARCH APPROACH HUMAN NATURE METHODOLOGY		Actors Approach	

Fig. 7.6. Ontological Considerations in the Actors Approach

Note that the paradigms SO1, S1, and S2 stand for the relative positions of these paradigms on the objective-subjective continuum. In other words, you should read the figure as follows:

▶ Paradigm SO1 represents the middle position on the subjectivist end of the continuum. It is the same paradigm in figure 7.5.
▶ Paradigm S1 represents the next position on the subjectivist end of the continuum.
▶ Paradigm S2 represents the extreme subjectivist position.

KEY POINTS

This chapter highlights the importance of philosophical assumptions underlying every research project. Your task is to reflect on the root assumptions that you are making in your project. The following points should guide you in defining the philosophical assumptions:

▶ Each of the paradigms described in this chapter considers some research issues to be more important than others; thus, the choice of paradigm influences research issues and vice versa.
▶ You must reflect on the assumptions underlying the theories that you consider appropriate as reference points for your own study. Such reflections will improve your understanding of the theories.
▶ Examine the degrees of consistency between your own assumptions and those held by authors of the theories that you use in the project. Where discrepancies are noted, you must discuss the implications of such discrepancies for your investigations.
▶ Do not see the paradigms as religious doctrines. They can be combined under given situations, but you must explicitly justify the combinations that you propose in your study.

PART 3
METHODS AND TECHNIQUES

If empirical investigations are required to answer your research questions, you will need to choose among the various types of data collection methods and techniques found in social science. Your choice of methods and techniques must, however, be consistent with the research approaches that you have adopted. Textbooks on research methodology group data collection methods into two broad categories: 1) *qualitative* methods and 2) *quantitative* methods. Each group of methods is designed to help researchers achieve specific research goals. Some textbook authors will suggest to you that you should choose either one of the two sets of methods, based on your preferred way of understanding the social phenomenon that you want to investigate (i.e., your choice of paradigm). Other authors argue that elements in both sets of methods can be combined to provide a better insight into the issues that you are investigating. To be able to make a good choice, you need to understand the similarities and differences between the two sets of methods. The aim of this part of the book is to provide you with this understanding.

Chapter eight introduces you to the methods and techniques that are frequently used to collect qualitative data. A similar introduction to quantitative methods and techniques is provided in chapter nine. Chapter ten discusses the possibilities of mixing both methods, while chapter eleven provides a summary of the key points in the book.

CHAPTER 8
QUALITATIVE DATA COLLECTION METHODS AND TECHNIQUES

Introduction

Qualitative research methods have increased in popularity among social science researchers during the last three decades. This chapter introduces you to the general characteristics of these methods and techniques. It also draws your attention to some of the challenges you should be aware of when you decide to use them, and what you should do to strengthen the quality of your work.

GENERAL CHARACTERISTICS OF QUALITATIVE METHODS

The term *qualitative method* is generally used to represent a wide variety of data collection methods. These include ethnography, participant observation, in-depth interviewing, and conversational interviewing (Bryman and Bell, 2011). Strauss and Corbin (1998: 10–11) define qualitative research as "any type of research that produces findings not arrived at by statistical procedures or other means of quantification". Such types of research are described as emphasising "cases and contexts"; that is, they engage in detailed examination of cases that are related to their chosen topics and present "authentic interpretations that are sensitive to specific social-historical contexts" (Neuman 2006: 151).

Box 8.1 provides an example of a project in which a student decided to use qualitative methods for the data collection. As the description in the box shows, a key advantage of using qualitative data collection methods is that participants (i.e., those you study) are often interviewed and observed in their natural settings. They may thus be able to more accurately answer questions about their settings. In other words, if you choose to use qualitative data collection methods, you must design your research in a way that enables you to get a firsthand look at the settings in which those you study operate and see what the participants describe in their answers. Qualitative methods also allow the participants to raise topics and issues that you may not anticipate and that might be critical to the investigation. Furthermore, they allow participants to express their feelings and offer their perspectives in their own words. In other words, if your study is concerned with gaining newer insights into the phenomenon that you are investigating rather than finding confirmation for existing theories, you must strongly consider using qualitative methods to collect your data.

Box 8.1. Understanding Intercultural Interactions within Danish-Vietnamese Joint Ventures

The objectives of this student's project were to understand:

1. How Danish and Vietnamese managers interact in joint ventures located in Vietmam and how their cultural backgrounds influence the interaction processes, and
2. How their interaction processes result in dynamic changes in the culture of the joint ventures over time.

The study was inspired by the *social constructivist* paradigm (Burrell and Morgan, 1979) combined with *symbolic interactionism*. That is, the student held the view that culture is continuously negotiated and constructed by interacting individuals.

The student's initial literature review revealed that no previous study was conducted in Vietnam on the subject, while limited empirical investigations were done on Danish joint ventures in countries other than Vietnam. But none of these studies adopted a social constructivist perspective on culture. The study was therefore designed to gain deeper insight into processes between Danes and Vietnamese rather than to test a particular set of hypotheses.

In order to establish consistency between the student's paradigmatic preference and the research objectives, the student adopted a qualitative approach to data collection. She collected her data

> through in-depth interviews as well as observations (she worked in two of the joint ventures for a combined period of six months). The data were presented in the form of narratives and analysed using qualitative data analysis software called Nivo.

QUALITATIVE DATA COLLECTION TECHNIQUES

The three commonly used techniques in qualitative data collection are:

▶ Focus groups
▶ Observations
▶ Qualitative interviews

Focus Groups

The *focus group* technique allows you to bring a selected number of people together to discuss the issues that your investigation centres on. For example, if a company is about to introduce a new product into a particular market and is not sure about how consumers will respond to the product and marketing strategies, the company may ask you to conduct a focus group study to gain insights into potential consumer perception. To do this you will select about twelve individuals who do not know each other. Your selection should be guided by some specific criteria (e.g., age, income, and levels of education) that are of particular interest to the company. You should then arrange with them to meet and discuss various aspects of the product—quality, colour, size, price range, and typical shops in which such a product will be expected to be sold.

This session typically lasts for one to two hours. You will act as a facilitator of the discussion, while the participants will be required to engage in a free discussion of the issues that you consider important for your investigation. The free discussions allow them to explore and clarify their views in ways that would be less easily accessible in one-to-one interviews. As a facilitator, you are expected to ask probing questions when necessary, in order to stimulate the discussion. You will usually bring someone along to take notes while the discussion goes on. The sessions may also be videotaped, if the participants agree to such an arrangement. When group dynamics work well, a focus group session will provide new and unexpected perspectives on the marketing strategies that the company might have been contemplating adopting.

The insights provided in the focus group discussions may provide a sufficient empirical base for your project report. If you consider it insufficient, you may combine it with other types of data.

Observations

When you are dealing with a subject that people are likely to feel uncomfortable or unwilling to discuss you may want to use observations as part of your data collection technique. You may use your observations simply to describe the phenomenon (i.e., write down what you observe) or to make inferences about what you observe, or even make personal assessments. For example, you may be able to observe what people are doing and through these observations make inferences about their attitudes, based on behaviours that they exhibit. But since you may be wrong in your inferences and evaluations, it is a common practice to engage in dialogue with those you observe (i.e. conduct qualitative interviews with those under observation) in order to check the accuracy of your inferences.

Observation studies are of two basic types: nonparticipant and participant. If you are a *nonparticipant observer*, it means that you visit the people you observe but do not take part in their daily activities. This makes you a "stranger" to the environment and therefore you "intrude" on the situation that you observe. Your presence may therefore make the observed situation less normal, since the participants will be aware that they are being observed and alter their behaviour accordingly. Such a technique may be necessary, if you (as an observer) do not have competencies required to participate in the daily work process of people you observe. For example, if you are observing nurses at work, you may not be able to participate directly in their actual nursing process unless you have the training and competencies to do so.

Participant observation studies, on the other hand, require you to become an active participant in the environment in which the study is conducted. You will do exactly what those you observe do and record your observations in the process. You will usually engage in informal conversations with other participants as part of the data collection process.

When you use a participant observation method, you will need to spend several days (and maybe months) with the participants in the research project. For example, if you are doing an investigation in a company, you will need to observe the employees of the company while they are working, engage in small talk with them, take notes of what you hear in the corridors and canteens, et cetera. If you are invited to sit in on some of their meetings, this will provide you with a good opportunity to gain first-hand impressions of how decisions are made. You will also be allowed to supplement the information you get from these observations and conversations with written documents from the company and formal interviews with some key employees.

The advantage of using the participant observation method is that it gives you a profound understanding of the setting within which the research is done. This will enable you to provide a description of the context within which the participants operate.

The most obvious difficulty with participant observation is that you cannot avoid becoming involved with the group at a social and emotional level. This may well influence your own behaviour and change the very phenomena under study. In other words, participating in the group activities may make an unbiased collection of data difficult. You may be able to reduce the bias when you deliberately record your observations frequently and reflect on what you observe. You must not rely too much on your memory. Record your observations at the end of the day or week.

If you serve as an intern with an organisation, participant observation becomes one of the useful data collection techniques you must consider. The same holds true for those of you doing your studies on a part-time basis while working. If your research is done in a company where you work, the participant observation method will definitely be a useful data collection method you must consider.

Remember that it takes a long time and a lot of effort to collect data using observational methods. Participants' behaviours must be observed over a long period of time for you to be able to make reliable inferences. Furthermore, as a researcher, you cannot be everywhere at all times. What you observe is therefore a snapshot and partial evidence of what actually happens. You must therefore be careful in making generalizations on the basis of your observations.

Qualitative Interviews

Interviewing is another technique you can use to collect qualitative data. As we can see in chapter nine, interviewing is used in collecting quantitative data as well, but there are differences. Qualitative interviewing seeks to gain an insight into the lived experiences of the person you are interviewing. It provides you with the opportunity to listen to what respondents themselves say about issues that you investigate in their own words. It can be used alone in collecting the required data, or in conjunction with other qualitative data collection techniques.

One of the most popular techniques in qualitative interviewing is the *critical incident technique* (CIT). This is a useful technique in gaining insights into people's experiences and the impact of such experiences on their perceptions and behaviours. Flanagan (1954: 333) described the critical incident technique as "an observable human activity that is sufficiently complete in itself to permit inferences and predictions to be made about the person performing the act". The technique is composed of two facets: 1) the critical incident itself and 2) reflections. The critical incident may be a snapshot, a situation, or an encounter that the person has been engaged in. The reflective component involves engaging with and exploring the incident with the person that you are interviewing on both intellectual and emotional levels. The aim of the reflection is to reach a new understanding of the experience with the person.

CIT allows the people you interview to freely describe their experiences and unreservedly express their feelings, and to reflect on their experiences while they are talking to you. In this way you and the respondent will be able to explore new dimensions in your investigation.

You will usually start the process by asking the respondent to describe some critical incidents that he or she experienced personally in the field of activity being analysed. The respondent then narrates the event naturally just as he or she would in a conversation with friends or acquaintances. They may not remember the events in chronological order and may go back and forth in narrating thier experiences. Allow them to do so, and take notes as they speak. You may tape the interview if the respondent allows you to do so.

Such an interview may take several hours at one go, or several days with short interviews per day. But in the end, you will come out with a richer understanding of the person's lived experience and gain more insight into the subject of your investigation.

CHALLENGES IN COLLECTING QUALITATIVE DATA

Those of you who consider statistical methods to be difficult may want to choose qualitative research method in order to avoid the statistics. Others may consider qualitative methods to be a lot easier and less time consuming. Basing your choice on these motives would be a mistake. In fact, qualitative methods are difficult to use. As noted above, the methods require you to seek an understanding of the social phenomena you investigate through the voices of those you investigate. In its pure form, this means that you should avoid imposing preconceived ideas on your data—you would not usually start your research with a theoretical understanding of the phenomenon you seek to analyse. Instead, you will spend much time on your data analysis and let your understanding emerge from the data. This approach is referred to as *inductive research* in the literature (Denzin and Lincoln, 2003). This means the theories you discuss under your literature review will basically provide you with a preunderstanding of the issues you seek to investigate (see Bryman and Bell, 2011). You will then use the qualitative data you collect to analyse the extent to which the existing theories explain the issues you investigate and at the same time produce new insights that emerge from the data. Getting good results from qualitative data thus requires substantial skill and experience.

Your personality and the personality of those you study also have some influence on the data you are able to collect. The personalities may influence the extent to which deeper meanings and feelings are explored and revealed through interviews. Some of you may be hesitant to press further for richer insights. In some situations, those you interview may be guarded in their responses.

There is also the question of the validity of your investigations. How can you be sure that you have not misunderstood what you have observed, or have provided a misinterpretation of what you have been told by your respondents? Can you be absolutely sure that those you interview are honest in their narrations?

EVALUATION OF QUALITATIVE STUDIES

The discussions above raise the issue of evaluation. Qualitative studies are usually evaluated on the basis of: 1) trustworthiness and 2) authenticity (Silverman, 1993; Bryman and Bell, 2011).

Trustworthiness is assessed in terms of the following dimensions:

- ▶ *Credibility*: This examines the extent to which you have followed the accepted procedures in conducting qualitative investigations.

Usually, you must send your interview transcripts to your respondents for them to confirm that you have correctly understood what they have told you. In other words, your research will achieve greater credibility when your respondents have validated the data you have collected. This is referred to as *respondent validation*.
- *Transferability*: This requires you to provide a detailed account of the context within which your study has been conducted. This will enable future researchers to compare your study with theirs in order to determine whether your findings hold true in other contexts.
- *Dependability*: This requires that you keep detailed records of all phases of the research process: problem formulation, selection of research participants, fieldwork notes, interview transcripts, et cetera. These materials will provide evidence that you have done the study in the prescribed manner. In other words, the dependability criterion reinforces credibility and transferability criteria.
- *Confirmability*: This requirement adds further weight to the three previous criteria of trustworthiness. It requires you to demonstrate that you have acted in good faith all along in the research process. In other words, you do not have any other interest in the research than to understand the reality that you set out to investigate.

The second evaluation criterion, *authenticity*, relates to the extent to which your investigations are fair (i.e., include all relevant people and their viewpoints), improve understanding of the social phenomenon that you seek to investigate, and provide opportunities for those involved to improve their insight into their own situations and act to change them, if they deem it necessary to do so.

KEY POINTS

If you define your research task to be one of uncovering meanings rather than testing pre-established hypotheses you must strongly consider adopting qualitative data collection methods. This method allows you to focus on a participant's own understanding and interpretations of their situation.

The three qualitative data collection methods that you may consider using are the following:

▶ A focus group
▶ Observational methods
▶ Qualitative interviewing (especially CIT)

A focus group method can be used as a primary source of data, or combined with two or more data gathering methods. Observational methods are useful when the subject of investigation is sensitive and people are reluctant to talk about it, or when the issues under investigation can be observed through people's behaviours. The critical incident technique is a useful source of data when the participants in the investigation can identify the events or circumstances that led to the critical incident and when the factors that make the event critical can be identified.

You should not choose qualitative methods and techniques because you think that they are simpler to use than quantitative methods. Qualitative data collection and analysis are more time- and resource-consuming than most quantitative methods. You should choose them when they are consistent with your view of the social phenomenon that you want to investigate (i.e., your problem formulation and paradigmatic preferences).

CHAPTER 9
QUANTITATIVE DATA COLLECTION METHODS AND TECHNIQUES

INTRODUCTION

If you seek to test specific hypotheses or find numerical answers to specific elements in your research questions, you may strongly consider using quantitative data collection methods. There are a variety of quantitative data collection techniques that you may consider, but this chapter introduces you to the two most popular ones: questionnaire-based surveys and interviews. The chapter also provides you with an overview of the general characteristics of quantitative data collection methods and guides you in writing good questionnaires and conducting interviews to gather quantitative data.

GENERAL CHARACTERISTICS OF QUANTITATIVE METHODS

Quantitative data collection methods allow you to test hypotheses derived from theories you have read about the issues you are investigating in your project. Such studies will usually encourage you to investigate causal relationships between specified variables. In other words, your theories will indicate that some specific variables influence other variables to produce an effect.

Let us take an example of a study of youth performance in schools in a given county in Denmark. Let us assume that you are interested in understanding why some young people within the age group of fifteen to twenty in county A do less well in school than young people in a similar age group in county B. You will need to identify which variables have been found in previous studies (e.g., in other counties) to influence young people's performance in classes. You will then want to test whether the previously identified variables impact performance of the young people in the county in which your study is conducted.

Let us take another example. If you are interested in differences in the performance of companies in Denmark, you will have to identify measurable indicators of company performance (e.g., profitability or market growth rate) and identify factors that impact company performance. You will then collect quantitative data from a number of companies to determine whether the relationships identified in previous studies hold true in your study as well.

Quantitative methods are generally less flexible than qualitative methods. There are standardised procedures and techniques for collecting, organising, and analysing the data. These standardised and well-accepted procedures tend to accord quantitative methods with a scientific image and make them very popular in social science research. The systematic and standardised data collection procedures also allow you to collect data that are sufficiently general and make the results of your investigation generalisable.

Box 9.1 provides you with an illustrative example of objectives and research design for a quantitative study. In this example, a student wanted to investigate the manner in which foreign students adjust to a new culture and learning situation and how they manage possible stress factors in their new environment. The study was conducted among foreign students at Aalborg University.

> **Box 9.1. Acculturation and Stress Management among Foreign Students in Denmark**
>
> A student studied how foreign students in Denmark adjust to their learning situations and manage stresses associated with studying in a foreign country. The specific objectives of this study were stated as follows:
>
> 1. To identify adjustment challenges that foreign students face in a new learning environment;

2. To determine the extent to which programmes designed by university authorities to facilitate foreign students' acculturation processes have been successful in achieving the desired goal; and
3. To investigate the extent to which relationships between local students and foreign students promote mutual learning between the two grops.

The student conducted a review of previous studies showing that the degree to which foreign students adjust to their learning environment will depend on the following set of factors:

- Degree of similarity of host country culture and home country culture,
- The age and gender of the foreign student,
- The personality of the student, and
- The length of time the foreign student plans to study in the host university.

The student therefore considered it appropriate to use a quantitative method for the study and collected his data using questionnaires and structured interviews. The data were analysed using various statistical tools.

STEPS IN QUANTITATIVE DATA COLLECTION

Steps in the survey research process are outlined in figure 9.1. They start with defining the survey objectives, and continue with developing a sample frame, specifying the strategy for data collection, and conducting the appropriate analyses, as well as evaluation. Each of these steps is critical to the success of the survey. You must therefore take a holistic approach to the survey design by consciously considering all aspects of the survey process.

The steps outlined here build on the steps in the overall project work process presented in chapter three (see fig. 3.1 in chapter three). Your definition of the survey objectives in the data collection phase must be consistent with your problem formulation, as well as the theories, concepts, and models that you have discussed earlier in the project. You will also derive your hypotheses from your literature review and theoretical discussions.

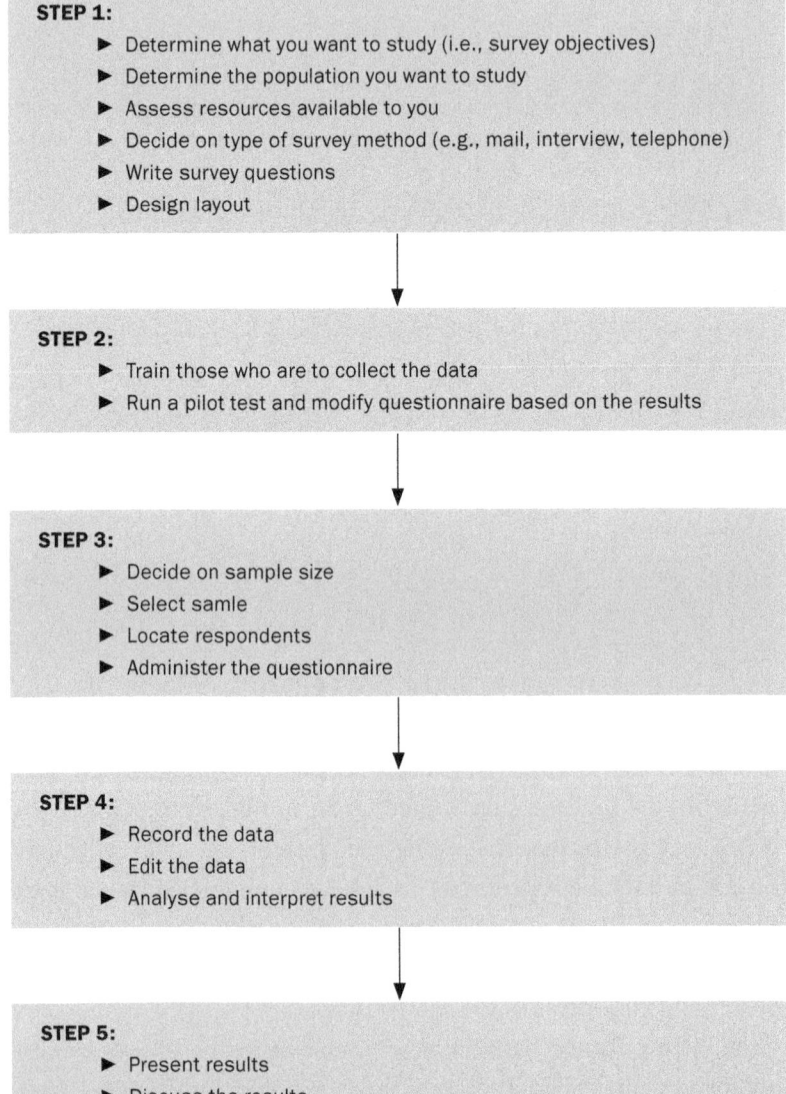

STEP 1:
- Determine what you want to study (i.e., survey objectives)
- Determine the population you want to study
- Assess resources available to you
- Decide on type of survey method (e.g., mail, interview, telephone)
- Write survey questions
- Design layout

STEP 2:
- Train those who are to collect the data
- Run a pilot test and modify questionnaire based on the results

STEP 3:
- Decide on sample size
- Select samle
- Locate respondents
- Administer the questionnaire

STEP 4:
- Record the data
- Edit the data
- Analyse and interpret results

STEP 5:
- Present results
- Discuss the results

STEP 6:
- ▶ Use findings to write your draft report
- ▶ Present findings to others for critique and evaluation
- ▶ Write final report based on feedback from your supervisor and peers

Fig. 9.1. Steps in the Process of Survey Research (Source: Based on Neumann 2006; Brymann and Bell 2011).

QUANTITATIVE DATA COLLECTION TECHNIQUES

You can use different techniques in the data collection process. The main ones include surveys and interviews.

Questionnaires

A questionnaire is the most conventional data collection instrument used in surveys. Writing questionnaires is, however, not as easy as you may think. It requires practice, patience, and creativity. You must make sure that respondents perceive the questions to be clear, relevant, and meaningful. The same words may convey different meanings to different respondents. This is particularly a problem in cross-national research situations where respondents are likely to have different frames of reference. Furthermore, the fact that respondents participate in surveys out of kindness rather than economic rewards means that questionnaires must be attractive for them to bother to fill them out and and return them. Without treating questionnaire design in a professional manner, an analyst would risk a low response rate. The overall requirement in questionnaire design is that it must be respondent-friendly. Box 9.2 gives an example of a study where the student found it useful to use a questionnaire.

Box 9.2. Guidelines for Writing Good Questionnaires

1. You may structure your questionnaire as follows:
    Section 1: Information to fulfil basic objectives of the study
    Section 2: Information to fulfil other research objectives
    Section 3: General opinion information (if needed)
    Section 4: Identification (i.e., demographic data of the respondent)
    Section 5: Thank you statement
2. Your initial questions should be captivating, general, clearly stated, and easy to answer. Place difficult questions towards the end of the questionnaire.
3. All questions on a particular topic should be grouped together and in a logical fashion before the questionnaire moves on to another topic.
4. Keep your questions brief, and the questionnaire itself must be short.
5. Make sure that there are no misspellings or grammatical errors in the questionnaire.
6. Avoid controversial, embarrassing, or emotionally charged questions as much as possible. If these are absolutely necessary, place them towards the end of questionnaire.
7. Consider placing demographic and lifestyle questions toward the end of the questionnaire. Some respondents are uncomfortable with such questions, but are willing to provide the information after going through the other questions.
8. Avoid double-barrelled questions. A double-barrelled question is the type that requires the respondent to address more than one issue at a time.
9. Avoid leading or loaded questions. A leading or loaded question is the type that directs the respondent to give a specific answer.

Source: Based on Shao (1999); Neumann 2006

There are two types of questions that you may ask respondents to answer: 1) closed and 2) open-ended questions. A closed question is one that can be answered with either a single word or a short phrase. Examples include questions seeking demographic information, such as age, sex, levels of education, and marital status of respondents. Closed questions are easy to answer and can be answered quickly.

If your respondents are not well educated, it may be a good idea to make most of the questions closed since this will make it easier for them to complete. It will also be easier for you to code and analyse closed questions than open-ended ones.

Open-ended questions normally demand long answers. Some of them require the respondent to think and reflect on specific situations or events before answering them. In this way, respondents may provide more nuanced insights into the phenomenon you seek to investigate. On the other hand, open-ended questions are more difficult to code and analyse.

Your questionnaire must be accompanied by a covering letter that introduces the potential respondent to the research project, stresses its legitimacy, and encourages participation. When you plan to administer the questionnaire to the respondent yourself, send a covering letter to the respondents prior to the face-to-face contact. This will help you break the ice and create a good atmosphere for the interaction during your meeting with the respondent. Remember the following points when writing your covering letter:

▶ Address the letter to the specific prospective respondent.
▶ Use your university's professional letterhead stationary.
▶ Specify the general topic on which you are conducting your investigation and stress its importance to the prospective respondent.
▶ Give assurance that the prospective respondent's name will not be revealed.
▶ Communicate the overall time frame of the study to the respondent to solicit his or her involvement. This should also include the completion date for the questionnaire.
▶ Communicate where and how to return the questionnaire.

▶ Provide an advance thank-you statement for willingness to participate.

Administering Questionnaires

There are various methods of administering questionnaires. These include mail, online, or by the researcher. The factors you need to take into account in deciding on the appropriate method include the objectives of the study, the sample and its geographical distribution, the types of questions, the resources at your disposal to do the research, as well as cultural and behavioural tendencies among the respondents.

Administering through Mail

Mail surveys are self-administered questionnaires (i.e., the respondents fill in the questionnaire themselves). By using the mail survey technique, your respondents (i.e., those who provide you with the data) can do so without revealing their identity. This will allow them to respond with openness and to sensitive questions. Mail surveys also avoid interviewer bias and are relatively cheap compared to interviews. You do not have to arrange meetings with each individual respondent. If you have a limited research budget and want to collect data from many respondents, you must seriously consider mail survey. But in countries where mail systems are not very reliable, this technique may be less appropriate.

Furthermore, if respondents are not particularly interested in the subject matter, most of them may fail to respond, and the survey may suffer from low response rate. The mail survey approach further denies the analyst the rich information that may be gathered through interviews (allowing respondents to clarify their answers) and observations.

Online Surveys

The development and pervasiveness of Web technology in developed countries now provides a cheaper and speedy technique for conducting surveys. Estimates show that the use of online survey technique can reduce costs by twenty to forty percent and provide the results in half the time it takes to do traditional mail surveys. Furthermore, if you use the online survey technique, you can increase your sample sizes without corresponding cost increases. For example, those groups of professionals (e.g., doctors and top-level executives) who find it difficult to allocate time to interviews may be willing to respond to online surveys that they consider relevant, but at their own convenience. In addition to this, it will be easier for you to send reminders to respondents through electronic mail and time them to arrive during the less busy time of the day. You can also more readily analyse the results of online surveys.

Quantitative Interviews

As noted in chapter eight, you can collect qualitative data through interviews. You can also collect quantitative data using interviews. Interviews can be conducted in two main ways: 1) either through face-to-face interactions or 2) through telephone or video-based interactions. The main advantage of telephone interview is that the respondent can give his or her answers anonymously.

The first step in an interviewing process is respondent selection. If you are collecting data from companies and institutions, you can select your respondents in a combination of two ways: 1) as a representative of an organisation and/or 2) as a private individual. The mode in which respondents are selected influences the content of their response. Respondents who are selected as representatives of their respective organisations tend to speak *for* their organisations, representing an official or public face. Respondents who are selected in their individual capacities speak *of* the organisations and on other management issues in general, and may tend to be more critical and open in their views.

The manner in which questions are asked during an interview process will determine whether the respondents reply either for their organisations or talk of the organisations. The interviewer must therefore be mindful of the changes in orientation made by the respondent during the interviewing process.

Another important problem faced in the respondent selection process is the potential censorship built into the process. This relates to the requirement in many organisations that top managers must approve of the respondents selected. There is, therefore, the danger of indirect data censorship in the sense that management may restrict the coverage in order not to expose what they consider to be bad sides of the organisation.

Selection bias may, however, be an outcome of necessity. It is natural to expect that the most detailed information is obtained from those respondents who are willing to share their thoughts and feelings with the interviewer about different situations within the organisation, and have the time to do so in detail. It is always difficult to find many of those people within an organisation. It is therefore not unusual for interviewers to select their respondents on the recommendations of those they have interviewed earlier. In situations where respondents are selected through recommendations of previously interviewed respondents there is a danger that the chain of selection becomes friends of the initial respondents or friends of their friends. In this way, the sample becomes purposefully selected rather than reflective of the entire spectrum of the organisation. This can weaken the validity of the accounts they give as representing an overall perspective of the organisation.

Types of Interviews

Interviews are classified into two groups: 1) standardised interviews and 2) nonstandardised interviews. *Nonstandardised* interviews may be either semistructured or in-depth interviews. *Standardised* interviews are normally used to gather data, which will then be the subject of quantitative analysis. Nonstandardised interviews serve the purpose of gathering data for qualitative analyses. As Saunders *et al.* (2007: 313) explain it, "these data are likely to be used not only to reveal and understand the 'what' and the 'how' but also to place more emphasis on exploring the 'why'". Standardised interviews use a questionnaire-type format. Some scholars refer to them as *interview-administered questionnaires* or *quantitative research interviews* to indicate that they are largely used in connection with surveys. The interviewer reads each question to the respondent and then records his or her responses on a standardised schedule, usually with precoded answers. Structured interviews have all the advantages of questionnaires. They also carry the benefit of the interviewer clarifying any question on the list that the respondent may have difficulties in understanding. Interviews also provide respondents with the opportunity to reflect on events without needing to write anything down. The face-to-face interaction with an interviewer also gives the respondent some degree of confidence to divulge sensitive information. Not many people are willing to fill out questionnaires and provide sensitive information to people that they have never met, even if assurances have been given by the researcher that the responses will be treated with anonymity.

In *semistructured* interviews the researcher will have a list of themes and questions to be covered. The questions may, however, vary from one interview situation to another. The order of questions may also be varied depending on the flow of the conversation. The variations allow the researcher to introduce additional questions where relevant in order to explore specific dimensions of the research question in specific interview situations, such as where the respondent has special or expert knowledge to share on specific issues.

Unstructured interviews are much more informal than semistructured interviews. Researchers use them to gain deeper insights into general areas of research interest. There are no predetermined lists of questions. The respondent is permitted to take control of the conversation and may digress into areas that he or she considers relevant. The interviewer must, however, possess substantial interviewing skills in order to keep the respondent from deviating too far from the central issues of the investigation.

The semistructured and unstructured interviews are recommended where the researcher is undertaking an exploratory study or a study that includes an exploratory element. They allow the researcher the opportunity to probe into issues that he or she may not be immediately aware of and therefore may not be able to capture by available theoretical knowledge.

Interviewing creates data quality problems. Common among them are different forms of bias, issues of validity, and generalisability. Respondents normally construct and uphold an image or front in relation to the interviewer. As long as they treat the interviewer as a stranger, the information they give will be influenced by this natural caution. Respondents may feel the need to conceal information if they consider its disclosure to be injurious to their career prospects in the organisation. The reality they present through their responses can therefore be a distorted one.

It has also been suggested that interviewers with limited experience can create situations that produce biases in the interview process. These include their body languages and the sequencing of the interview. These biases are particularly very potent in semistructured and unstructured interview situations.

The psychological atmosphere of an interview is, thus, at least as important as the mechanics of the interviewing process. When the interviewing context is felt by respondents to be permissive and relaxed, his or her desire to censor the information they provide will be greatly reduced. Effective interviewing therefore requires insight into the dynamics of interaction. Interviewers are advised to adopt styles that strengthen rapport and goodwill.

EVALUATING QUANTITATIVE STUDIES

Reliability here relates to dependability or consistency (Neuman, 2006). If other students and researchers under identical or similar conditions can repeat your research process, it will be judged to be reliable. Reliability in this connection is evaluated on three dimensions:

- *Measurement reliability*: This assesses to what extent the variables are measured in a consistent manner.
- *Stability reliability*: This assesses the extent to which the measurement of the variables produces consistent results at different points in time.
- *Representative reliability*: This assesses the extent to which the measurement of the variables yields consistent results for various groups of respondents.

KEY POINTS

Quantitative data collection methods and techniques are generally used by researchers that subscribe to an objectivist view of reality and positivist epistemology. This allows them to formulate and test hypotheses, and to arrive at results that are generalizable; thus, if your project seeks to produce generalisable knowledge, you must seriously consider using quantitative data collection methods.

There are specific steps and standard procedures that you must follow when collecting quantitative data and some of them have been presented above. There are also various statistical software packages that you can use in analysing quantitative data. You must seek the advice of your supervisor on which packages are available at your university.

CHAPTER 10
MIXED RESEARCH METHODS

INTRODUCTION

Your choice of data collection methods must always be guided by your problem formulation. You must use the methods that provide the best opportunities for answering research questions. Some research questions are best answered by using quantitative methods, while others require the use of qualitative methods. An increasing number of researchers, however, consider a combination of quantitative and qualitative methods to provide the best insights into several different social science problems. But simply using qualitative and quantitative methods in the same study without thoughtful integration or explanation does not add substantial value to an investigation. The aim of this chapter is to introduce you to the advantages and disadvantages of mixed methods and how to go about using them.

First, I summarise the similarities and differences between quantitative and qualitative data methods to enable you to do a quick comparison between the two sets of methods. I then describe the viewpoints that may guide you in your decision to mix the two methods and how to combine them.

SIMILARITIES AND DIFFERENCES BETWEEN QUANTITATIVE AND QUALITATIVE METHODS

Table 10.1 provides you with a summary of the main differentiating characteristics of quantitative and qualitative research instruments. It shows that the perspective you adopt in a particular research will determine whether your investigation must be done with quantitative or qualitative methods.

Let us take the example of a study in which you are interested in investigating the use of information technology in an organisation. You may choose to emphasise the process of adoption of the information technology and the meanings that employees associate with the technology. Such a focus will suggest the use of qualitative method since this will help you gain insight into the symbolic meanings that workers assign to the information technology through their daily interactions and communication. In this case you will be adopting a constructivist and interpretivist paradigm to your study. On the other hand, if your research concerns the types and amounts of data that a company collects from its customers by using various types of computer software, you may be inclined to adopt a quantitative method.

QUANTITATIVE RESEARCH	QUALITATIVE RESEARCH
Test hypothesis that the researcher begins with	Capture and discover meaning once the researcher obtains the data
Concepts are in the form of distinct variables	Concepts are in the form of themes, motifs, and taxonomies
Measures are systematically created before data collection and are standardized	Measures are created in an ad hoc manner and often specific to the individual setting or researcher
Data are in the form of numbers from precise measurements	Data are in the form of words and images from documents, observations, and transcripts
Theory is largely causal and used deductively	Theory can be causal or noncausal and is often used inductively
Procedures are standard and replication is frequent	Research procedures are particular and replication is very rare
Analysis proceeds by using statistics, tables, or charts, and relating them to the hypotheses	Analysis proceeds by extracting themes or generalisations from evidence and organising data to present a coherent and consistent picture

Table 10.1 Some General Characteristics of Quantitative and Qualitative Research (Source: Based on Silverman, 1993; Neuman, 2006; Bryman and Bell, 2011)

MIXING QUANTITATIVE AND QUALITATIVE METHODS

Mixed methods research is generally considered to be a third set of data collection methods. They are therefore described separately from either quantitative or qualitative methods, and require careful integration. Truscott *et al.* (2010) argue that the goal of mixed methods is not to replace quantitative or qualitative approaches, but to draw from their strengths and minimise their limitations. Similarly, O'Cathain *et al.* (2007) argue that mixed methods research is more than mixing different methods; it is a purposeful and powerful blend intended to increase the yield of empirical research.

Before you decide on using both quantitative and qualitative methods in your study, you must reflect again on your paradigmatic preferences. If we follow Rossman and Wilson's (1985) classification of researchers, ask yourself whether you are a purist, a situationalist, or a pragmatist (see chapter five above). If you consider yourself a purist, this means you will reject the combination of quantitative and qualitative methods in a single research study. As argued in chapters five and eight, a purist will consider paradigms to be incommensurable. If you are a situationalist, you will consider quantitative and qualitative methods to supplement each other. You will therefore be willing to combine both sets of methods in situations were you consider the combination to provide the best results. If you are a pragmatist, you will use methods that you consider to be convenient for a given project, bearing in mind the objectives of your study, as well as your resource limitations. In other words, you will choose the method that works best for you, regardless of any philosophical or paradigmatic assumptions. You will therefore be willing to use a combination of quantitative and qualitative methods if you find such a combination feasible under the circumstances in which your research is done. In other words, it is only the purist that will reject mixed research methods.

Following Green *et al.* (1989), mixed methods will enhance your research in five major ways:

- *Triangulation* helps to test the consistency of your findings by using different methods.
- *Complementarity* allows you to clarify and illustrate your results by using different methods, and providing different perspectives on the issues you have investigated.
- *Development:* using different methods will enable you to incrementally build on the results obtained from one method by the use of subsequent methods or steps in the research process.
- *Initiation:* different methods will help bring up new research questions or challenges.
- *Expansion:* you will obtain greater richness and detail in your study by exploring specific features of each method.

Thus, by using mixed methods, you will be able to use pictures and rich narratives to add meaning to statistical information in your study. Alternatively, you can provide numbers to add precision to your narratives and pictures. In other words, the strengths of one method can compensate for the weaknesses of another.

The following steps should guide you in your decision and use of mixed methods:

1. You must convince yourself that a mixed method is appropriate for your research before you decide to use it. This means that you must provide a justification for using mixed methods in the methodology chapter of your project.
2. You must carefully and deliberately decide on the types of methods to use and the sequence in which they will be used in your project. For example, if you decide to observe the people that you study, interview them, and send them questionnaires to fill out, you must decide on the order in which the different data collection methods will be used and provide reasons for the sequence that you have chosen.
3. Collect the data using the different methods, noting the difficulties you face in the data collection process.

4. Validate the data using the various approaches outlined in chapters eight and nine.
5. Use the data to write your report and reflect on the limitations to your findings (if any) resulting from the data collection methods that you have used.

TRIANGULATION

Triangulation is another common term used in the literature to refer to mixed methods. As Jick (1979) observes, triangulation allows the researcher to improve the accuracy of his or her conclusions by relying on data from multiple methods. But triangulation means more than mixing methods. Denzin (1978) identifies four types of triangulation:

- Theoretical triangulation
- Data triangulation
- Investigator triangulation
- Methodological triangulation

Theoretical triangulation is similar to the multiple paradigm approach discussed earlier. In Abnor and Bjerke's terminology, theoretical triangulation allows the researcher to construct his or her *operative paradigm* in a way that accommodates two or more metatheoretical perspectives (Arbnor and Bjerke, 2009). These perspectives will then guide data collection and analysis. Hassard's (1991) study—presented in the next section—is an example of such a study. Students are very often encouraged to engage in theoretical triangulation by combining theories that (together) provide a more useful understanding of the phenomenon they choose to investigate.

Data triangulation is a data collection strategy that derives data from multiple sources or samples. A business student who collects data from different segments of consumers and channel members is invariably engaged in data triangulation. In this regard, many eclectic models that guide researchers to seek information about different dimensions of a social phenomenon may be said to motivate the adoption of data triangulation.

Investigator triangulation refers to the use of more than one investigator (i.e., observer, interviewer) or coder and data analyst in a single study. The collected data is considered more credible when those collecting the data have not had prior discussions with each other about the subject of investigation or collaborated in any other way during the data collection process.

But the most common use of the term triangulation in the literature is what Denzin (1978) refers to as *methodological triangulation*. It has two forms: 1) within-method triangulation and 2) between-method triangulation. When the researcher uses different techniques within the same method it is a *within-method* triangulation. When different methods are employed in the same research (e.g. quantitative and qualitative methods) it is labled *between-method* triangulation.

Some researchers use the term *multiple triangulation* to describe research strategies that use two or more of the categories of triangulation listed above.

Triangulation as a research methodology has been criticised by several social science researchers. Deetz (1996), for example, argues that to assume that different research methods simply provide additive insights into the same phenomenon is an illusion. The thrust of his argument is that the modes of analysis do not work from different points of view on the same thing; they are producing and elaborating in the act of researching different phenomena for different reasons.

EXAMPLES OF MIXED METHODS

Mixed methods are now increasingly used in social science studies and there are many scholars who argue in support of this approach to research. For example, Gioia and Pitre (1990) argue that social science scholars are best served by mixed methods, since this will help them capture the dynamic complexity of social phenomena. In the same vein, Deetz (1996) suggests that communication across methods and research approaches is necessary in social science research, since societies are complex and people with different worldviews help build the world together. Schultz and Hatch (1996) also suggest that different research approaches and methods operate as complements by revealing sequential levels of understanding within an integrated research project. These scholars therefore suggest that the use of mixed methods may entail the endorsement of multiple paradigms in single research projects.

One of the most frequently cited studies that have used multiple approaches is that by Hassard (1991) who studied the work behaviour in a division of the British Fire Service. His research strategy consisted of four different approaches described by Burrell and Morgan (1979): functionalist, interpretive, radical humanist, and radical structuralist approaches (see chapter seven). Since each of the four approaches considers some research problems to be more important than others, Hassard modified the focus of his research questions to correspond to the concerns of the various approaches at various stages of the research. A functionalist approach inspired the first part of the study, which focused on how firemen assessed the motivating potential of their jobs. To do so he collected quantitative data using the job diagnostic survey instrument developed by Hackman and Oldham (1980). The second part of the study relied on an interpretive paradigm in order to gain insight into how routine events in the Fire Service were accomplished in a context of uncertainty that stemmed from the constant threat of emergency calls. He collected the data for this part of the study by asking the firemen to describe and explain their daily tasks in their own words. The third part of the study adopted a radical humanist paradigm. The objective of this part of the study was to understand how management training in the Fire Service contributed towards the reproduction of an ideology that supported and reinforced capitalist values. The fourth part was based on a radical structuralist paradigm and focused on the development of employment relations and conflicts over working time. In this way, he was able to use four different approaches in a single study.

KEY POINTS

Mixed methods provide you with a third method of data collection—quantitative and qualitative methods being the other two sets of methods. Before deciding on using mixed methods, you must make sure that you are true to your paradigmatic preferences. If you consider yourself a purist (i.e., you believe strongly in some specific philosophical assumptions about how to do social science research) you may consider not using mixed methods. Those of you who subscribe to the advantages of crossing paradigms may consider mixed methods a research approach that produces richer insights into your study.

Remember that mixed methods do not mean simply using qualitative and quantitative methods in the same study. Its usage requires clear justification and thoughtful integration. You must therefore provide good reasons for adopting this approach in your project.

CHAPTER 11
SUMMARY, REFLECTIONS, AND FURTHER READINGS

INTRODUCTION

The main objective of this book is to provide you with an understanding of some of the challenges that you are likely to face in writing academic projects and to guide you to use the experiences as important inputs in your overall learning process. This last chapter revisits some of the points made in the previous chapters and summarises them for your quick overview and reference. It also suggests additional readings for you. These additional references should enable you to gain more comprehensive knowledge about some specific issues discussed.

The summary follows the issues discussed in the previous ten chapters chronologically.

PROBLEM FORMULATION OR RESEARCH QUESTIONS

The first task you must engage in when writing a project is to define the research questions you want to address. This is also referred to as problem formulation. The problem formulation defines the focus of the project and guides the overall research design. It also shapes the expectations of the readers and examiners of your project. You must therefore give adequate attention and time to this task.

Clarity and precision are essential requirements for good problem formulation. There is a tendency for some students to attempt to formulate their research questions too broadly for fear of not covering the core issues in their subjects. Others tend to have multiple objectives for their projects. You must avoid falling into such traps. You can do so by taking a look at some of the best projects written by past students of your programme and discussing your problem formulation with your supervisor and classmates.

Working in groups enables you to discuss your viewpoints with your colleagues and to combine your respective strengths to write a good project. But group work has its own challenges due to the personality differences and the different roles that the group members tend to play. You must be tolerant and work towards group synergy, since this will enhance your overall performance as a group.

PROJECT STRUCTURE AND STYLE OF WRITING

Structure and systematic presentations are important ingredients in writing a project. If the structure of your project is good, it will provide your readers with a compass that helps them follow the chronology of your thinking and the logic underlying your arguments. You must therefore think through the general sequence and flow of your thoughts when designing your project.

Your writing style—the manner in which you express your thoughts—is also important. It will enhance the clarity of your arguments and the overall quality of your project. You must always remember that the goal of writing the project is to communicate to your readers. To do so effectively, you must write simple and short sentences. You must also avoid borrowing vocabularies and terminologies that you do not understand simply to make your work appear academic.

LITERATURE REVIEW AND THEORIES

A critical review of the existing literature in your subject area is essential for you to write a good project. The literature review offers you the opportunity to demonstrate your knowledge of theories, models, and evidence found in the literature and to select those you find particularly useful to your own study. The review therefore enables you to ground your research in available contemporary knowledge. A good review will help you do the following things:

▶ You will identify theories and models that are currently used by other researchers in the field.
▶ You will be able to summarise what is known and what is not known with respect to the issues that you are interested in, and thereby help justify your own research.
▶ You will be able to identify areas of controversy in the literature and present your views on these controversies.
▶ You will be able to discuss the strengths and weaknesses that you find in the theories, with particular reference to your own research questions.

PHILOSOPHY OF SCIENCE AND ITS INFLUENCE ON YOUR PROJECT

The discussions of philosophy of science (chapter seven) show you that there are a wide variety of ontological assumptions underlying studies that social scientists undertake. Good knowledge about these assumptions will help you specify the philosophical foundation (i.e., *paradigm*) on which your study should be based. The paradigm you choose, which reflects basic beliefs about reality, ways of knowing, human nature, et cetera, will influence your overall research strategy. For example, if you subscribe to a *positivist* view of reality you will most likely adopt a causal research strategy. Your data collection and analysis will aim at understanding the variables that shape the phenomenon you investigate and the links between them. On the other hand, if you choose an *interpretive* paradigm, you will see reality that you investigate as socially constructed, and you will find qualitative approaches to be more appealing.

Some scholars suggest that all social science research, to some extent, is subjective. For example, Jenks (1993: 49) argues that "objectivity in social science does not constitute the establishment of absolutely 'correct' facts, but the reflexive assurance of the selection of the same facts for all practitioners. Objective knowledge is, therefore, intersubjective—it is part of a social context that is always its object of concern". If you subscribe to Jenks's argument, you will be inclined to combine objective and subjective perspectives in your research by adopting a situationalist view of paradigms (see chapter five and ten for elaboration).

METHODS

The discussions in chapters eight to ten show that the methods used in research unavoidably influence the objects of inquiry. For this reason you are advised to provide a clear account of the process of data collection and analysis in the methodology chapter of your project. Although such detailed accounts add to the length of the report, they also allow the readers to judge whether the findings reported are adequately supported by the data. This will further reinforce the validity and quality of your study.

SELF-ASSESSMENT AND REFLECTION

It is advisable that you allocate some time at the end of the project for self-assessment and reflection. You must carry out a self-examination of what has worked and what has not in the project that you are about to submit. Such a self-assessment of the project serves a number of purposes. First, it helps to improve the project. Second, it helps you to reflect on the limitations that cannot be remedied before the submission. By doing so, you become aware of the shortcomings of the project and can therefore prepare more effectively for the oral defence (if required). Third, it helps you to identify ways in which the project can be taken further either by yourself in the future or by other researchers.

Some of the following questions may guide you in your self-assessment process:

- ▶ What has been the overall goal of this project?
- ▶ Have you succeeded in capturing the reader's interest in the introduction and concluding parts of the project?
- ▶ Have you been successful with your research?
- ▶ What do you like best about the project?
- ▶ Which chapters do you assess to be strong?
- ▶ What do you like least about the project?
- ▶ Which parts can you still improve, and what will the incremental value of the improvement be?
- ▶ Is there a common thread holding the various chapters of the project together?

FOR FURTHER READING

All the references cited in the previous chapters provide rich sources of additional knowledge about the issues discussed in the book. In addition to them, you can gain further insights into some of the issues by reading the books listed below.

General Guidelines

Fisher, C. (2010). *Researching and writing a dissertation: An essential guide for business students*. Essex: Pearson Education.

- ▶ This book is well structured and easy to read. It provides a step-by-step guide to business students on how to build their dissertations. It includes guidelines on how to refine a research topic and write critical literature reviews. It also contains discussions about the criteria used by examiners in their assessment of dissertations.

McBurney, D.H. and T.L. White (2009). *Research methods*. Belmont, CA: Wadsworth/Cengage Learning.

- ▶ This book also provides a logical, step-by-step guide through essential stages of the research process: selecting the project, searching for literature, research design, implementation, analysis, and report writing.

Hart, C. (2005). *Doing a literature review: Releasing the social science research imagination*. London: Sage Publications.

▶ The book offers students a practical and comprehensive guide to writing a literature review. It takes the reader through the initial stages of an undergraduate dissertation or postgraduate thesis.

Philosophy of Science

Psillos, S. and M. Curd (2008). *The Routledge companion to philosophy of science*. Abingdon: Routledge.

▶ This is one of the most recent books on philosophy of science. It provides comprehensive insight into themes, movements, debates, and topics in philosophy of science. It introduces the reader to some of the leading concepts, thoughts, and debates on the subject, as well as the historical and contextual background of these thoughts.

Rosenberg, A. (2005). *Philosophy of science: A contemporary introduction*. Abingdon: Routledge.

▶ This is another book that students keenly interested in philosophy of science can benefit immensely from reading. It takes the reader through issues such as the relationship between science and philosophy, science and western civilization, definitions, explanations, causations, and laws, as well as fundamental questions raised in science and philosophy today.

Methods

Strauss, A. and J.M. Corbin (1998). *Basics of qualitative research:*

Techniques and procedures for developing grounded theory. London: Sage Publications.

▶ The book introduces the reader to how theories can be developed on the basis of qualitative research (as compared with quantitative research). They also discuss some of the commonly asked questions about grounded theory methodology and provide some answers. The book also provides a detailed description of qualitative coding and analysis techniques. It is most useful to researchers who already have good insight into grounded theory and seek to extend their knowledge about how to use the approach.

Silverman, D. (2010). *Doing qualitative research.* 3rd ed. London: Sage Publications.

▶ It is a well-structured and easy-to-read book that discusses the do's and don'ts in qualitative research. Students who have limited knowledge about qualitative research will find the book highly useful.

Yin, R. (2004). *The case study anthology.* London: Sage Publications.

▶ This book introduces readers to the current state-of-the-art in case study research. It covers issues such as case selection methods, analysis of case data, multiple case methods, and the use of quantitative evidence in case studies.

Yin, R. (2009). *Case study research: Design and methods.* 3rd ed. London: Sage Publications.

▶ Yin's book is the most comprehensive presentation of the design and use of the case study method as a valid research tool to date. It is widely read by students and scholars interested in case methods. The author discusses the debate between qualitative and quantitative research and the challenges of data triangulation in research.

BIBLIOGRAPHY

Abnor, I. and B. Bjerke (2009). *Methodology for creating business knowledge*. London: Sage Publications.

Allaire, Y. and M.E. Firsirotu (1984). Theories of organizational culture. *Organization Studies*, 5(3): 193-226.

Andersen, H. (1990). *Videnskabsteori og metodelære*. Gylling, Denmark: Samfundslitteratur.

Baxter, P. and S. Jack (2008). Qualitative case study methodology: Study design and implementation for novice researchers. *The Qualitative Report*, 13(4): 544-559.

Belbin, R.M. (1981). *Management teams: Why they succeed or fail*. Oxford: Butterworth Heinemann.

Belbin, R.M. (1993). *Team roles at work*. Oxford: Butterworth Heinemann.

Berger, P. and T. Luckmann (1967). *The social construction of reality*. New York: Anchor Books.

Blumberg, B., C.R. Donald and P.S. Schindler (2005). *Business research methods*. 2nd ed. Boston: McGraw-Hill Higher Education.

Blumer, H. (1969). *Symbolic interactionism: Perspective and method*. Berkeley: University of California Press.

Bryman, A. and E. Bell (2011). *Business research methods*. 3nd ed. Oxford: Oxford University Press.

Burrell, W.G. and G. Morgan (1979). *Sociological paradigms and organizational analysis*. London: Heinemann.

Butterfield, L.D., W.A. Borgen, N.E. Amundson and A.-S. T. Maglio (2005). Fifty years of the critical incident technique: 1954-2004 and beyond. *Qualitative Research*, 5(4): 475-497.

Chandler, A.D. (1962). *Strategy and structure: Chapters in the history of the American industrial enterprise*. Cambridge, MA: MIT Press.

Crewswell, J.W. (2003). *Research design: Qualitative, quantitative, and mixed methods*. Thousand Oaks, CA: Sage Publications.

Crotty, M. (1998). *The foundations of social science research*. St. Leonards, New South Wales: Allen and Unwin.

Cyert, R.M. and J.G. March (1963). *A behavioral theory of the firm*. 2nd ed. Englewood Cliffs, NJ: Prentice Hall.

Deetz, S. (1996). Describing differences in approaches to organization science: Rethinking Burrell and Morgan and their legacy. *Organization Science*, 7(2): 191-207.

Deetz, S. (1999). "Multiple stakeholders and social responsibility in the international business context: A critical perspective". In P. Salem (ed.), *Organization communication and change: Challenges in the next century.* Cresskill, NJ: Hampton Press: 289–319.

Denzin, N.K. (1978). *The research act.* New York: Wiley.

Denzin, N.K. and Y.S. Lincoln (1998). "Introduction: Entering the field of qualitative research". In N.K. Denzin and Y.S. Lincoln (eds.), *The landscape of qualitative research: The theories and issues.* London: Sage Publications: 1-34.

Denzin, N.K. and Y.S. Lincoln (2003). *The landscape of qualitative research.* 2nd ed. Thousand Oaks, CA: Sage Publications.

Fast, M. and W.W. Clark (1998). *Interaction in the science of economics* (unpuplished monograph). Aalborg: Centre for International Business, Aalborg University.

Fisher, C. (2010). *Researching and writing a dissertation.* 3rd Edition Essex: FT Prentice Hall.

Flanagan, J.C. (1954). The critical incident technique. *Psychological Bulletin,* 51(4): 327-358.

Fletcher, D. (2006). Entrepreneurial processes and the social construction of opportunity. *Entrepreneurship & Regional Development,* 18(6): 421–440.

Gioia, D.A. and E. Pitre (1990). Multiparadigm perspectives on theory building. *Academy of Management Review,* 15: 584–602.

Granovetter, M. (1985). Economic action and social structure: The problem of embeddedness. *American Journal of Sociology,* 91(11): 481–493.

Greene, J.C., V.J. Caracelli and W.F. Graham (1989). Toward a conceptual framework for mixed-method evaluation design. *Educational Evaluation and Policy Analysis,* 11(3): 255–274.

Gullestrup, H. (2006). *Cultural analysis: Towards cross-cultural understanding.* Copenhagen: Copenhagen Business School Press.

Hackman, J.R., and G.R. Oldham (1980). *Work redesign.* Reading, MA: Addison-Wesley.

Hart, C. (2005). *Doing a literature review: Releasing the social science research imagination.* London: Sage Publications.

Hartley, J.F. (1994). "Case studies in organizational research". In C. Cassel and G. Symon (eds.), *Qualitative methods in organizational research: A practical guide.* London: Sage Publications: 208–226.

Hassard, J. (1991). Multiple paradigms and organizational analysis: A case study. *Organization Studies,* 12(2): 275–299.

Hofstede, G. (2001). *Culture's consequences: Comparing values, behaviors, institutions, and organizations across nations.* 2nd ed. Thousand Oaks, CA: Sage Publications.

Jenks, C. (1993). *Culture: Key ideas.* London: Routledge.

Jick, T.D. (1979). Mixing qualitative and quantitative methods: Triangulation in action. *Administrative Science Quarterly,* 24(4): 602–611.

Komives, S., Lucas, N. and T. McMahon (1998). *Exploring leadership for college students who want to make a difference.* San Francisco: Jossey-Bass Publishers.

Kuada, J. (1994). *Managerial behaviour in Ghana and Kenya: A cultural perspective.* Aalborg, Denmark: Aalborg University Press.

Kuada, J. and O.J. Sørensen (2000). *Internationalization of companies from developing countries*. New York: Haworth International Business Press.
Kuhn, T.S. (1970). *The structure of scientific revolutions*. Chicago: University of Chicago Press.
Lewis, M.W. and A.J. Grimes (1999). Meta-triangulation: Building theory from multiple paradigms. *Academy of Management Review*, 24(4): 672–690.
Mcburney, D.H. and T.L. White (2009). *Research methods*. Belmont, CA: Wadsworth/Cengage Learning.
Merton, R.K. (1968). *Social theory and social structure*. New York: Free Press.
Miles, M.B. (1979). Qualitative data as an attractive nuisance: The problem of analysis. *Administrative Science Quarterly*, 24: 590–601.
Meltzer, B. (2003). "Mind" in L.T. Reynolds and N.J. Herman-Kinney (eds.), *Handbook of symbolic interactionism*. Walnut Creek, CA: Alta Mira Press: 253-266.
Neuman, L.W. (2006). *Social Research Methods – Qualitative and Quantitative Approaches*. 6th Edition. Boston: Pearson Education.
O'Cathain, A., E. Murphy and J. Nicholl (2007). Integration and publications as indicators of 'yield' from mixed methods studies. *Journal of Mixed Methods Research*, 1: 147–163.
Parker, M., and G. McHugh (1991). Five texts in search of an author: A response to John Hassard's 'Multiple paradigms and organizational analysis.' *Organization Studies*, 12: 451–456.
Parsons, T. (1951). *The social system*. Glencoe, IL: Free Press.
Psillos, S. and M. Curd (2008). *The Routledge companion of philosophy of science*. Abingdon: Routledge.
Rossman, G.B. and B.L. Wilson. (1985). Numbers and words: Combining qualitative and quantitative methods in a single large scale evaluation. *Evaluation Review*, 9(5): 627–643.
Saunders, M., P. Lewis and A. Thornhill (2007). *Research methods for business students*. 4th ed. London: FT Prentice Hall.
Schultz, M., and M. J. Hatch (1996). Living within multiple paradigms: The case of paradigm interplay in organizational culture studies. *Academy of Management Review*, 21: 529–557.
Silverman, D. (2010). *Doing qualitative research*. 3rd ed. London: Sage Publications.
Shao, A.T. (1999). *Marketing research: An aid to decision making*. Cincinnati, OH: South-Western College Publishing.
Strauss, A. and J. Corbin (1998). *Basics of qualitative research*. London: Sage Publications.
Truscott, D.M.S., S.S. Smith, F. Thornton-Reid, Y. Zhao, C. Dooley, B. Williams, L. Hart. and M. Matthews (2010). A cross-disciplinary examination of the prevalence of mixed methods in educational research: 1995-2005. *International Journal of Social Research Methodology*, 13(4): 317–328.Weber, M. (1968). *Economy and society: An outline of interpretive sociology*. Berkeley: University of California Press.
Whitley, R. (2001). Developing capitalism: The comparative analysis of emerging business systems. In G. Jacobsen and J.E. Torp (eds.), *Understanding business systems in developing countries*. New Delhi: Sage Publications: 25–41.

Yin, R. (1994). *Case study research: Design and methods.* 2nd ed. Thousand Oaks, CA: Sage Publications.
Yin, R. (2004). *The case study anthology.* Thousand Oaks, CA: Sage Publications.

SUBJECT INDEX

A
Abnor and Bjerke's Three Methodological Approaches 84
Abstracts 47
Acronyms 48
Actionable knowledge 23
Active learning 19
Actors approach 88
A leader type 27
Analytical approach 85
Antipositivism 73
Authenticity 101

C
Classifications of paradigms 15
Collect qualitative data 15
Completer 29
Critical incident technique 98

D
Denmark 69
Descriptive research 42

E
Epistemological 15
Epistemology 59
Executive summaries 47

F
Focus group 95
Forming 31
Free-rider 30
Functionalism 76

G
Grand theory 65
Group studies 20, 22

H
Human nature 59

I
Ideographic 73
Inductive research 100
Initial Norming 31
Innovator 27
Integration of theory and practice 20, 23
Interactional functionalism 79
Internet source 52
Interpretive interactionalists 80
Interpretive paradigm 72
Interpretivism 77
Interviewing techniques 60
Interviews 60, 112
　Nonstandardised 112

Semistructured 113
Standardised 112
Unstructured 113

K
Knowledge creation 19

L
Levels of understanding 57
Literature review 40, 68

M
Mail surveys 110
Metatheories 64, 71
Methodology 59
Microtheories 66
Midrange theory 66

N
Nominalism 73
Nomothetic 73
Nonregular processes 86
Normative research 42
Norming 32

O
Observations 96
　Nonparticipant observer 96
　Participant observation 97
Online Surveys 110
Ontology 15, 58

P
Paradigm 71

Pedagogical approach 11
Performing 32
Philosophy of science 13, 71
Positivism 73
Positivistic paradigm 72
Pragmatists 61
Problem- and project-based learning 11
Problem formulation 21, 38
Problem-oriented studies 20
Project-organised teaching 20
Project work process 14
Purists 60

Q
Qualitative Interviews 98
Qualitative method 93
Quantitative data 103
Quantitative Interviews 111
Quantitative methods 15

R
Radical humanist paradigm 83
Radical structuralist paradigm 83
Realism 73
Regular processes 86
Research 14
Research design 14, 57
Research process 35
Research questions 36
Research strategy 41

S
Scandinavian approach 20

Situationalists 61
Social sciences 13
Sociology of radical change 81
Sociology of regulation 81
Structure your project report 14
Symbolic interactionism 88, 94
Systems approach 86
Static structures 86
Storming 32
Structural functionalism 78
Structural interpretivists 79
Structuralism 77
Supervisor 33

T

Team organiser 29
Theories 15
Thought Developer 28
Triangulation 121
   Data triangulation 121
   Investigator triangulation 122
   Theoretical triangulation 121
Trustworthiness 100